© Heikki Toivanen

2025

The Art of Teaming

From Hierarchy to the Team Learning Community

Illustration and layout: Timo Lehtonen

Translation: Tim Whale

Cover: Juho Sallinen

ISBN: 978-952-80-9657-3

Publisher: BoD · Books on Demand,
Mannerheimintie 12 B, 00100 Helsinki,
bod@bod.fi
Printed by: Libri Plureos GmbH,
Friedensallee 273, 22763 Hampuri, Saksa

TABLE OF CONTENTS

1. The team as a learning tool 5

2. Towards team-learning work communities 10
- Team Academy is a pioneer in education 10
- My own experiences with teams 14
- The coronavirus brought efficiency to meetings 17
- Changing mindsets 19
- Meaningfulness as drivers in work life 21
- A shared vision of teams is a driving force 23
- The learner at the centre of learning 27

3. Why a team is formed 31
- Co-operation is a human strength 31
- From fear to courage – From leader or teacher to team coach 31
- Learning together 34
- The learning team and project team 35
- Time 38
- Shared vision 40
- Rules of the game 40
- Team agreement 41
- Team coach 42
- Learning agreement – Your own life plan 42
- Literature related to your own learning 43
- Learning by doing 45
- A few empirical observations and book recommendations to assist you in rea-sing your dream 45
- Cultural change is a path of perseverance and determination 47
- Team learning is experiential learning 47
- Dialogue creates self-direction 50
- Epistemology – The theory of knowledge 52
- Organising team activities 54

4. Team coach and coaching leader 56
- New management models 56
- The difference between Team Coach and Coaching Leader 57
- Approval of multi-speeds 59

5. Team Coach Laws 61

- The Law of Non-Interference 61
- Slowness of Learning 62
- The Law of The Thin Red Thread 64
- Learning Environment Act 65
- The Law of The Team Coach's Own Role 67
- Customer Relationships Act 67
- Act of Interference 69
- The Law of Rhythm 70
- The Thinking and Preparation of the Team Coach 70

6. Socrates and team coach competencies 72

- Team Coach Competencies 73
- Be tough in the learning culture – but soft on people 75

7. The start is the most important stage 78

- The team is built on differences 78
- First encounter 81
- Team trust and communication 82
- Leadership and relevance? meaningfulness in a team 83
- Planning provides an effective start 85

8. Stages of team building 89

- Team stages 89
- Measuring team performance 95

9. The challenges and blues of teamwork 98

- Slow learners 98
- The twisted mindset of the whole team or Team Coach 101
- Special situations in the team 103
- Beating the blues 105

10. Bring your own character into play 108

- Every team coach and coaching situation is different 108
- Learning facilities, home and meeting points 110
- Awareness/perception/ Mindfulness – Emptiness 113

Acknowledgement

I am used to achieving things on time and with precision – I previously worked for the global paper machinery company Valmet in their paper machine operations for some 10 years. Valmet is renowned for its punctual and precise project work. This book project progressed in a completely reverse way. So much has happened in my life: I have been financially trapped in three different apartments, my businesses have had all kinds of joyful challenges or opportunities, and along with my wife we rebuilt a house originally built in 1902, with a sauna building in the garden, located on the Pispala ridge in Finland's third largest city, Tampere. In addition, I was succumbed to handle the repair work related to water damage at the local Dance Factory in Tampere. I also became a full-time father also coped with the extremely sad passing away of my little sister. Furthermore, I have had all kinds of other issues to manage, such as writing this book which has provided me with moments of pleasure. My life has been divided into eight different action areas, which have been too much. Therefore, completing this book was a significant challenge that I set for myself and achieved.

This book project began just as the corona virus arrived, and it was completed at the beginning of 2025. Personally, I realised the true value and importance of the book during the international Team Coach Boost in September of 2024. One participant asked me how they could start team learning. I got to work immediately and translated three pages of the book using Google's translator, and despite the imperfect translation they were truly grateful.

I am a Doctor of Industrial Economics and a Master of Workshop Engineering by qualification, and according to my own empirical observations, many educational institutions are managed like a functional engineering workshop. It is viewed that teachers and students are similar to production goods on the production line of learning. You are not encouraged to think with your own brain. If thinking were freed, better learning outcomes could be achieved in a cost-effective way. This is why the message of this book is: Person's own individual thinking must be liberated.

Thank you, Mr. Timo Lehtonen, for pushing me to finish this book by helping with the layout, illustration and printing. You are perhaps the most experienced and productive Team Coach in the world. Thank you, my dear wife Irina, and my dear son Hugo, for giving me the time and space to write a book in the midst of all the events and issues. Thank you Sirkka-Liisa Heinonen for persistent language revision with a dyslexic person. Thank you for the comments and support of the book, e.g. Juha Wirekoski, Niina Palmunen, Teppo Kettula, Olli-Pekka Heinonen, Chris Jackson and Milla Kinnunen. A big thank you to the founder of Team Academy, State Counsellor of Education Johannes Partanen – I am privileged to be able to work with you for better learning.

Pispala, Tampere, Finland 4.6.2025

Heikki Toivanen, Dr. Sc. (Tech.)

1. The team as a learning tool

Our customers were on the verge of bellowing at my colleague and I in unison:

"We do everything ourselves. Enough is enough! What do you coaches actually do?"

Internally, I was very satisfied: the customer was realising the essentials of team coaching and coaching leadership. The learner is the customer, who must understand they are to take responsibility for their own learning.

Outwardly, the situation seemed very problematic when it came to the entire extended management team of the organisation, which is some twenty persons. Disgruntled customers may not be satisfied, even if they learn. I managed to calm the situation down by promising a little more structure for the next day. In team coaching, the customer creates their own structure around the themes they have raised. Team coaches only create a safe space for dialogue and experimentation. Now, in my haste, I promised to bring themes for the following day, while the customer was fully engaged in their own hierarchical leadership.

It was an overnight training session which finally ended up in the sauna. Purposefully, our days are long and include informal learning in agritourism companies. At least it happened tonight, I mused. In retrospect, I wondered if the decision was the correct one – should I have let the customer solve the situation themselves? On the other hand, I needed to create a safe environment, and I succeeded in that. I remembered the words of Brené Brown:

If you're comfortable, I'm not teaching and you're not learning. It's going to get uncomfortable in here and that's okay. It's normal and it's part of the process."

On the second day, the atmosphere was more sympathetic, but I am not sure if the participants are learning the correct things. It was a six-month process training, after which I admitted to the external client that I had not fully succeeded in this process. In spite of this, or precisely because of it, the client wanted to continue working with us. The client was actually satisfied with the learning process.

The customers also wanted to move away from the hierarchical management model. The model was developed during industrialisation in the early 1900s. At that time, only management had the knowledge needed for leadership, and only they had sufficient training for leadership. Nowadays, information is available to everyone. The artificial intelligence will make the knowledge available for everyone. Now, the employees of work communities are as educated or even more educated than managers. The hierarchical management model needs to be abandoned, and decision-making must be transferred to the members of the work community. Decision-making must take place in teams. Teams are the decision-making unit of future work communities.

I am a mechanical engineer by training. For the first fifteen years of my career, I worked in industry. And for the past fifteen years, I have coached work companies. I find it confusing how they have copied operating models from machine shops. Many communities are still run today just as Henry Ford ran his automobile factory in the early 1900s. In many companies, leadership is based on hierarchy and orders.

Unlearning the hierarchical leadership model does not mean chaos. This structure is pyramid-like, and the decision-making power lies with leaders. In the team-learning leadership model, the decision-making power sits with teams, in that it is structurally flat and thus equal. First, of course, the team and community must be of the right size to function: a maximum of 20-25 teachers or experts and 200-300 students. In a larger unit, people no longer know each other. The team of the community of experts should also be of the same size. One supervisor is able to lead and coach two teams. When the work community grows to the size of more than 25 employees, a new unit and team must be established.

I have read in several sources that a unit of 200-300 people is the maximum size for a community where everyone knows each other. My own observations support this. In Oulu in Finland, the Ritaharju School was built on this principle. The school has about 1400 pupils, but the school consists of a separate five units. Each unit with 200-300 pupils and about 25 teachers operate quite autonomously under the leadership of a team coach or a pair of team coaches. The management of Ritaharju School also works on the principle of pair management – the principal and the assistant principal run the school together. The correct structure is the starting point for building a culture of team learning.

In a team learning community, regular dialogue, i.e. genuine discussion, must be maximised. It is at the heart of the leadership model. Dialogue requires a lot of time, which is why teams need to reserve several hours a week for it. The third point is the common goal, i.e. a shared vision. A clear goal and rules for a team-learning work community must emerge from the work community. These form the structure of the work community. Moving from a hierarchical leadership model towards the power of teams enables team learning. In the same way, the teacher must relinquish their own power and transfer the responsibility for learning to the learners. It requires talent to build a team learning culture. When the learners and the team have responsibility, the team coach, i.e. the leader or teacher, must be careful about the correct type of learning culture.

The formation of the team and the development of its shared vision required leadership and team coaching. This is the reason behind the name of this book: The Art of Teaming. The Finnish translation of Teaming is Tiimistyminen which is a newly created word in the Finnish vernacular, which was developed during the process of book writing? In my own thoughts, the teaming means "A managed process of team formation, where learning, leadership, a shared vision of the team and the autonomy of the team are combined". In my opinion, team building is "team building that originates from the team, takes place without leadership and without a shared vision".

To create the correct kind of learning culture, you require:

1) The correct team and community size.
2) Regular sessions of dialogue.
3) Shared vision.
4) Interdependence of the team.

Team building requires team coaching expertise. A team needs a team coach who develops its self-management, or in fact, co-management. Team members guide and lead the team together. A team can also have a coaching leader, i.e. a team leader, just like a sports team has a coach and a captain. In a team, the individual learns faster than working individually, because the team acts as a learning mirror of the individual.

Team learning is considered to probably be the oldest form of learning among humans. Around campfires, deep in the past, hunter-gatherers would have shared their thoughts about the previous day's hunt and planned tactics for the next day's hunt. They learned co-operation through hunting and discussing their hunting. Back in those days no written information existed. Today, the amount of information is so vast that is it beyond the control of individuals. Different people have the necessary knowledge which when combined makes great wisdom in the team.

Greek philosophers developed a deeper word for campfire discussion which is dialogue. The word dialogue comprises of two Greek words dia and logos, which mean through, and the act of speaking, thus in total meaning through the act of speaking. The participants in a dialogue do not choose a side but think together with others. The dialogue and learner-based learning method of team learning is based on the fact that the team is a tool for individual learning. The team becomes a community of trust from which the learner receives feedback from their peers. An active learner acquires new skills and knowledge in interaction with team members, by reading theoretical information for their own needs and by experimenting with what they have learned. Team learning is a holistic learning method that combines action, feelings, sensory perceptions, bodily experiences, thinking together, reading and recording one's own goals. In a team, an individual learns many times faster and more efficiently than alone.

This book has varying perspectives, theories and stories that will provide you with inspiration for teamwork. Teamwork and learning exist in the middle ground between so many different human sciences that there is no single theory. Creative entrepreneurs of the modern era, such as Grace Beverley from England or Perttu Pölönen from Finland, are prime examples of this. They have the admirable courage of people in their young mid '20s to share a solid personal view of entrepreneurship, learning or the future. Their books are read by millions. Solid academic research, on the other hand, is often slow and cautious, and it does not provide a grip or help for the future. This book is based on my personal views, experienced theories and experiences. Team learning has been tested for more than thirty years, which means the slate is already well chalked.

We at Team Academy Global Ltd. (Tiimiakatemia Global Oy) have coached more than 2 000 team coaches in long-term coaching, with the method being applied in more than 20 countries.

In this book, I use the term team coach. A team coach has their own team or teams that they individually coach. A team coach can be a trainer, teacher, leader, director, manager, supervisor, expert, entrepreneur or even a coach. Ever increasingly, I meet people who are simply called team coaches. I use the term learner for the team member itself, because the focus of this book is to view the team as a tool for learning.

The second chapter of the book discusses team learning, and why a culture that learns as a team is required. The third chapter dives into the principles of team learning. The fourth chapter discusses what it means to be a team coach and a coaching leader. The fifth chapter highlights the importance of building a team culture. The sixth chapter examines the team's development stages and learning journey, because team coaches must understand the greater picture of teamwork. The seventh chapter discusses the challenges and dark sides of teamwork that a team must go through in order to develop. In the last chapter of the book, I reflect on the character of a team coach, because each of us is different and we must act through our own strengths. We refer to this as the team coach's character, i.e. the strengths of nature.

It is my belief that the terms team and the coach are the most misused terms that exist today. It would be more suitable to use the terms group and trainer respectively. A team differs from a group in that the team has a shared vision, a common agreed goal. The team meets regularly. The team is a suitable size. A group is a group of people who are aware of each other. The coach starts with the needs of the learner and is aware of the necessary relating information. The trainer only starts with the information that the learners may need. If in a "learning situation" the "coach" has more than 20 percent of the voice, he or she is a trainer, and it is a training event. The team can be used as a tool for organisation, as a tool for learning, or as a combination of these. When the team is used as a tool for learning, it is team learning. The team coach guides the learning process of the team.

The team has a separate team leader and team coach. The team leader, i.e. the leader of the team, is responsible for the team's operational activities and management. The team coach coaches the team. In much the same way as in sports, there is a team captain, i.e. a team leader, and a team coach, i.e. a coach for the team.

It is my belief that educational institution is a gloomy term. I have observed that renewal unfortunately often occurs either in terms of the structure of the building(s) or the finances. Buildings are erected that are excessively large, resulting in the educational establishment becoming a faceless school machine where learning is taylorised. Let us imagine that when teacher-led information is fed into the learner's head, learning would occur. It is now time for educational institutions to renew themselves and transform into communities of collaborative learning, i.e. team learning.

The same type of need for renewal exists in companies and other communities. Leadership must be reformed to meet the demands of new generations for equality and respectful leadership.

There are three key elements to a team learning community:

1. A shared vision, structure and operating culture of the entire community.
2. Functional teams, i.e. teams of a suitable size (maximum of about 25 people).
3. Communal or team learning, dialogue and learning by doing.

The most important feature in the background is trust. It is essential to create a safe atmosphere where mistakes can be made and rightly forgiven. Trust is born from openness and interest in other people. This book is aimed at reformers and learning leaders in work communities. The idea of the book is to offer practical thoughts and stories based on theory and my own empirical observations on how to transform a rigid organisation into a learning community. Finnish communities have already boldly embarked on the path to renewal. In this book, I share my own views, stories I have heard and personal experiences in the first person. In them, I combine my own memoirs, theories and teachings – some may even be misguided, or my accuracy in recalling the anecdote is lacking. The title of Henrik von Wright's (2002) memorial work, "My Life as I Remember It", should describe the veracity of these stories and theories. As a wise philosopher, von Wright ingeniously transfers the responsibility for understanding the book to the listener.

> *Once, a book-wise person who visited us at the Team Academy said: "This worked in practice, but how does it work in theory?"*

2. Towards team-learning work communities

Team Academy - A pioneer in learning

Peter Senge, a renowned developer of learning organisations, visited Team Academy in the 1990s and was amazed and he remarked: "The first true learning organisation in the world. Why are there so few of these?" I have heard and read this anecdote multiple times. I would have liked to have been involved back then, but I hadn't entered the team Academy arena by then. I was actually in Japan at the time. The establishing of the Finnish university of applied sciences system was also a distant thing for me. Johannes Partanen was looking to move from teaching, although his passion for learning was by no means waning. Above all, Johannes wanted to renew learning, and in his own words he misunderstood the idea behind the University of Applied Sciences. Much to the disappointment of Johannes, Universities of Applied Sciences became traditional bachelor's universities that implemented outdated pedagogy. His idea was to combine learning and business. His thoughts on this form of business model were modified, but Johannes thought that classroom number 147 would be similar to his own company and he would run it as if it were his own. Then both of his careers as a teacher and as an entrepreneur would be in symbiosis. The story goes something like the following: Johannes Partanen created a handwritten A4 advertisement and put it on the school bulletin board which read:

> "Do you want to go on a trip around the world and learn a little about marketing on the side? Come to classroom 147 on 19th January 1993 at 15.00."

Upon the door to the classroom the following notice was placed:

> "Be careful not to walk in, because your face will be grinning for the rest of your life!"

As many as 24 enthusiastic students expressed their willingness to enrol. Thus, on the 19th of January 1993, the first student team aptly labelled the "Round the Word Team" (RTW), was born. To the horror of the cleaners, all the desks were carried from the downstairs classroom of the school at Rajakatu 37 in Jyväskylä, Finland, to the corridor and people began to sit in a circle in comfortable armchairs like Native Americans around a campfire. In the early stages of the operation, Johannes brought the values that guided it to the students. These formed the values of the Team Academy. The values were learning by doing, practicality, continuous experimentation, continuous creation of new things, learning and travelling. The mission was to eliminate unemployment. The vision was the dream come true and create a job. The change was a matter of wanting to make a clear break and to break with traditional teaching, which is characterised by strict timetables and traditional classroom teaching, where students sit quietly and passively in classrooms listening to the teacher's lecture. The motto was placed on the classroom door:

The RTW team of students, or Round the World team, share the team's shared vision to travel around the world.

It sparked a new wave of enthusiasm at JAMK University of Applied Sciences. This team of 24 enthusiastic people, 12 young females and 12 young males, created a permanent new direction for Finnish organisational thinking and team learning. In the first team, about half of those who started went on to become entrepreneurs. Everyone on the team went on to successfully get a place of employment.

I have great respect for Johannes. A lot of his thoughts and reflections have been borrowed in this book. Johannes Partanen worked as a teacher at a Commercial College for the first 20 years. Johannes is a merited and experienced entrepreneur and teacher. He says that those years were spent growing into a good teacher. The following two decades, which he worked as the head coach and entrepreneur of Team Academy, were spent learning away from teaching and his creation of his own team coach.

Team Academy has been operating for now approaching some three decades, in which time real results have been achieved. Somewhere between 30 and 50 per cent of completed students become entrepreneurs (in contrast to the on average, three to five per cent from all universities). At best, tax revenues from the Team Academy (students) co-operative have covered the operating costs of the Team Academy. In addition to Finland, the activities have spread to twenty different countries. TAMK Proakademia of the Tampere University of Applied Sciences (TAMK) and Mondragon Team Academy of the Basque Country, who have taken inspiration from Team Academy, have been highly successful.

The team learning methodology is widely applied in companies, communities, comprehensive schools, vocational schools and higher education institutions. Experts, entrepreneurs and managers apply these methods in work communities. More than 2 000 people have completed the long Team Master training and more than 2 000 have completed the shorter Team Learning Start training. The method of team learning thus provides a very good basis for success in the complexities of modern working life.

The birth and development of the Team Academy has influenced numerous books and the theories that appear in them, which are described in Appendix One. British team coaches were able to compile a four-book series called Routledge Focus on Team Academy, which contains some 50 scientific articles about Team Academy. The first actual Team Academy book was published in 2002 (Niina Leinonen - Timo Partanen - Petri Palviainen). Johannes Partanen compiled the principles and models of team learning from the books and practical experiments that he had studied. Johannes described in his books The Team Coach's Best Tools (2012), Glimpses of Individual Learning (2014), What does a team coach need to know about innovation? (2019), Customer Focus (2022), Brand and Offering (2022), Sales and Marketing (2022) and Book of Books 2022-23 (2023) the principles of team learning.

Timo Lehtonen, a long-time team coach at the Team Academy, has written many excellent books on team learning methods, such as Team Academy, how to grow into a team entrepreneur (2012), Never Again Alone, I Do and Learn in a Team (2015) and Team Academy - How to Grow into a Team Coach (2022). The Digital brick and mortar shop as a hybrid of offline and online commerce (2019) by Timo is one of the best marketing books I have ever read. The author of this book has studied youth leadership as part of the TEKES Leader Programme and developed Johannes Partanen's theory of peer leadership in the Friend Leadership A Visual Inspiration Book (2014).

Learning by doing, reading and regular dialogue sessions are central to Team Academy. The idea is that each team learning community builds its own model of its own team learning. The rocket model developed by Johannes, which is used in the Team Academy of the Jyväskylä University of Applied Sciences, can be used as a basis, which is at the same time a model for creating team entrepreneurship and a study programme in business development. The rocket model has three tanks or lines: the Team, Customer and Individual Learning. In the middle and at the centre is the customer. On one side tank or line is the individual and on the other side tank or line is the team. The foundation of everything is formed by learning at the first level, the second level is management, the third is innovation and knowledge, and the fourth is the brand and offerings.

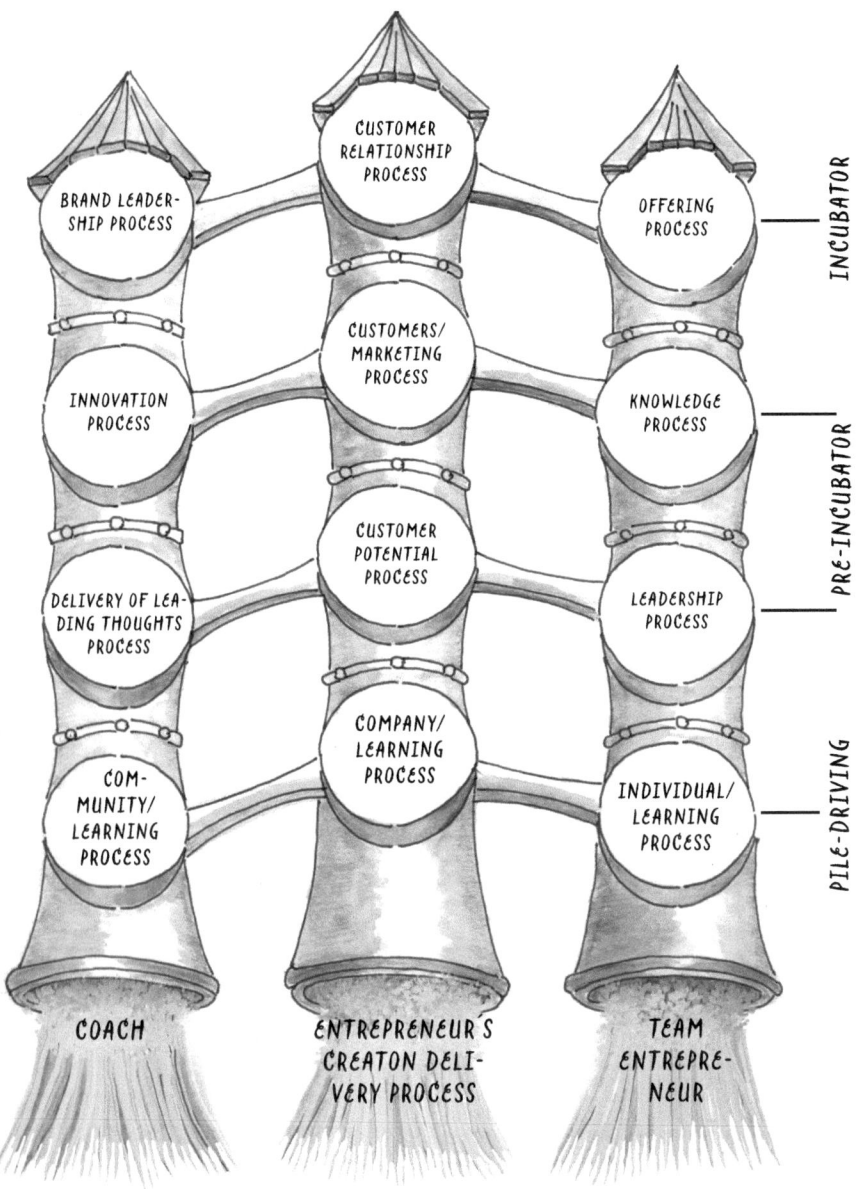

Figure 1. Rocket Model – Team Entrepreneurship Curriculum.

My own experiences with different teams

My life changed in 2008 when I began working as a team coach at the Team Academy of Jyväskylä University of Applied Sciences – I grew tired of the hierarchy and constraints of a large company and yearned for creativity, freedom and something invigoratingly new. It was a difficult point in my life: I took a long look at myself. I was accepted into the Team Master training organised by Partus Ltd, (Oy), which was a company founded by Johannes Partanen that became the Team Academy Global Ltd (Oy) and I found myself. I wanted to become an entrepreneur and a manufacturer. Owing to my qualification, I am also a M.Sc. (Tech.) in Mechanical Engineering, I started looking for machine shops and other industrial plants in the quest of becoming a manufacturer. After five years of searching, in 2014, Johannes asked me to be the CEO and brain manufacturer (shareholder) of Team Academy Global Oy. The beginning was particularly challenging. Team Academy Global Oy was at a crisis point which led me to put all my assets into loan guarantees and share purchases. For the following 3-5 years, we teetered on the edge of survival. Then we achieved a good position for many years until the present in 2024, when due to state cuts in education in Finland, we find ourselves once again facing new challenges.

Consciously building a top team is challenging. Only 5-10 percent of teams rise to the level of a top team. Building requires systematic work, the commitment of team members and the talent of successfully coaching a team coach. When you get to be part of a top team, you do not want to relinquish this position. The flow of work and making a result creates new results and a new enthusiasm. Difference, tolerance of differences and the development of team trust are required. A team is an effective learning environment. Even if it does not evolve into a top team, you learn more effectively as a member than on your own.

I have had the fine opportunity to be part of top teams a few times in my life. The first time I set up Savcor's business in Japan, where I, an enthusiastic engineer who had just graduated, along with an experienced Japanese businessman, who was just over 50 years of age, reportedly Masao Shiga, a member of the samurai family, formed a core business couple. He taught me business and civilised manners. We were complemented by Savcor's owner and CEO Mr. Hannu Savisalo, who supported us unreservedly in fair entrepreneurial spirit. Mayumi, our Finnish-speaking secretary, complemented our team by taking care of practical matters. We had no written team agreement or team rules. The goal of the unwritten team agreement was to establish Savcor's business in Japan and do our best at all times. Masao and I had a dialogue at least a couple of times a week over dinners. We reflected on our team's successes and planned the next steps. Hannu Savisalo visited Japan every two months. At this time, we reflect on the past and the future at dinners together. Mayumi was involved in them from time to time. During the working day in our small office, everyone was fully aware of the goings on at all times. We were a small project team of five. We were able to raise our business from zero to financially profitable in three years. Savcor is still operating today in Japan.

The second time I was part of a top team was when I got to work for the Paper Technology Company Valmet to create new business. I started the paper roll doctoring business as a Global Product Manager from scratch. Roll doctoring is the process of cleaning rolls by skilfully scraping the surface of paper machine rolls. After a few months of operation, I found out that the sales budget for the first year was a staggering one million Finnish marks, which equates to something in the region of more than one million Euros in today's terms. I was somewhat shocked because this was based on the sales expectations of a product that was actually still unfinished. After a hard struggle, I finally got the product to the trail stage on the world's fastest paper machine in Jämsänkoski, Finland.

I recall the customer saying about the product: "Nothing new, a little weaker than Pinaltek's products (Pinaltek was a competitor at the time). At least they have a new kind of logistic concept, which makes it much easier to handle the doctor blades."

Inspired by this feedback, I called Pinaltek's CEO. We get on well straight away. We organised a meet up and during our first meeting, I proposed that Valmet buy the majority stake in the company and that the CEO remains a minority shareholder. My supervisor at the time supported my plan unreservedly. This is how we became a core team of three. The business expanded into a significant size. The strength of our team was based on solid dialogue – we regularly spent sauna evenings together that were full of dialogue. We followed the principles of dialogue: we spoke directly, sometimes shouting, we respected each other, even though we were quite different. The first was Valmet's straightforward engineering director, the second was a business oriented determined entrepreneur, and I was the third, a slightly academic strategic leader who understood something about internationality. There was a little less listening and waiting – we acted immediately. This naturally resulted in a number of errors that we permitted.

I went to Italy on a so-called sales trip, but it became a wine and dinner trip – paper machines were too small and narrow for our service concept. I have ruined the market in Australia and built a useless recycled steel workshop in Germany. We succeeded in introducing a new doctoring blade material to the market, the only advantage of which was its cost-effectiveness. The doctor blade material itself did not work properly in cleaning the rolls. We allowed all these mistakes. On the other hand, we renewed the paper machine technology that was based on stainless steel by introducing composite structures. After the first trials, we launched completely new types of doctoring blade materials, composite doctor blade holders, and renewed the handling and logistics of sharp blades for factories. We became the market leader in a number of patents in our own operating area, which describes our success. I also accumulated about 20 patents – almost all of them invented together with the team. Our core team grew, and more top people joined it. This was a glorious period of time, but in a big corporation, organisations change.

I became the manager responsible for spare parts services for paper machines. Our Europe-wide branch comprised of some 50 persons. My supervisors were savvy, and I got help from four other managers, because managing a large unit required the creation of a different structure. We divided the staff of my department into four smaller groups, each of which was given its own area of responsibility. This is how hierarchies are built. The groups were formed from the point of view of organisation instead of learning. Connecting the learning and organisation of teams would require a different structure. I felt lost. Our team was still under construction when suddenly the organisation changed again.

The notion of writing a doctoral dissertation had crossed my mind on many occasions and for a long period of time. It was then that I met the most inspiring Professor Juha Näsi. I suggested to him that I would write a doctoral dissertation. He provided me with Henry Mintsberg's book The Rise and Fall of Strategic Planning and asked me to make an abridged version of it. I actually managed to get tired of I but Professor Juha Näsi accepted me as a postgraduate student. At the same time, I moved on to develop the global operations of Valmet. Soon I started preparing my doctoral dissertation on The Development of the Paper and Pulp Machine Industry from the 1970s to the 2000s in 2001 while working full time.

I was given study leave for 2005. The dissertation year was really inspiring. I woke up quite early in the morning, around five at the latest, and began writing. I was able to arrange interviews with the managers of all the key companies in the paper and pulp machine industry. My goal was to get to sit at Valmet's headquarters in my own chair. My professor and I did form a good team. He pushed me through the scientific pain. My goal of getting to the headquarters was not accomplished. However, Valmet went on to acquire the company Kvearner and in particular its boiler operations, which was thought to be based on the ideas presented in my dissertation. Then I returned to the roll doctoring business again and became its global leader. Then the organisation changed again. I became a person of wisdom in the global business arena, a kind of global sage. I soon became tired of hierarchical leadership and applied to go to Team Academy to be a team coach.

I went for an interview at the Team Academy of the JAMK University of Applied Sciences. I went with a document portfolio full of documents about my own life, such as photographs, books that inspired me, a doctoral dissertation and a master's thesis. The table was overflowing, to which Johannes Partanen was excited. This is how I became a team coach of the Team Academy. I got to coach. I thought I understood something about coaching leadership and team building. My theoretical understanding was quite limited, even though I had written a doctoral dissertation on strategy. It was then that I learned to really read. I learned to coach through mistakes. I became excited. I realised during the team training that I wanted to be a manufacturer, an entrepreneur and a CEO. Since I have a master's degree in mechanical engineering, I started looking for a suitably affordable machining shop company to buy as my own company. However, they were few and far between.

Johannes Partanen had founded Partus Oy at the same time as Team Academy started its operations. Until 2010, Partus, or Team Academy Global, coached entrepreneurs. The registered Team Academy brand had come into the possession of Partus Oy, because JAMK University of Applied Sciences did not want to continue the registration of the Team Academy name established back in the late 1990s. Since then, Team Academy Global Oy, a limited liability company, had focused on coaching team coaches. Unfortunately, sales and marketing were forgotten. Back in 2014, the company had run into a crisis – the previous CEO had left on a tight schedule. Johannes approached me and asked me to be the CEO. I accepted the offer. Before I started, I applied for my first cash loan, i.e. working capital financing, to secure the company's operations. At the time of applying for the second cash loan, I was also offered a large shareholding in the company.

This is how I became a brain construction manufacturer. Then the process of team building began. The number of employees in the company increased from three to five. Building a team does not happen quickly. It requires dialogue, considerable awareness and patience. Sometimes there are also mistakes in recruitment, as it is a top team where differences complement each other.

Coronavirus brought efficiency to meetings

Latte macchiato. I have two servings of it in my coffee thermos mug when I hastily make my way to my car at 6.45 in the morning. I have learned to first place the coffee mug in the cup holder in the car. Once I failed to follow this routine when I first put the coffee mug on the roof of the car and the other items things inside on the back seat. Of course, the result was that the full coffee mug fell from the roof and its coffee contents ended up on my suit jacket. I went to fetch a clean jacket. My planned morning changed in that I quickly made the decision to get the coffee soiled jacket laundered and, miracle of miracles, someone at the dry-cleaning company actually answered my call so early in the morning. In fact, this laundering experience resulted in me getting excellent customer service experience. I find myself entering the cleaning company's premises and I am able to take my jacket straight into the laundering area past the front desk service point. As I said, it was a miracle that someone answered the phone in the early hours of the morning and agreed to receive myself, the customer, bypassing the standard bureaucratic service process. My jacket is quickly accepted and goes directly to the laundry's production process. Humans are learners by nature, which is why we have learned to survive. People learn from other people.

I start the engine of the car. I head down the hill from Pyynikki to Pyynikintori in Tampere, Finland. It is quite early in the morning – a little before seven. I see Rellu, or Tampere Lyceum – a very beautiful, curved building. The rising sun makes the surface rugged and handsome. Frans Emil Sillanpää flashes through my mind, and his statue opens as a book in front of the Lyceum. In my mind, he represents an entrepreneur in the creative industries of the past, who left Hämeenkyrö in Fimland from humble circumstances and fought his way to become a Nobel Prize writer. I take a small dose of latte caffè macchiato – proper coffee. I am eternally grateful to my wife, who forced us to have Reinhard in our home as the third wheel of our marriage. I have named our Miele coffee machine Reinhard. Reinhard was one of the two founders of the home appliance company Miele.

I arrive at Pyynikintori. Tori means market in Finnish. This milieu is beautiful, even though all the parking spaces are full, as usual. The market square is surrounded by old apartment buildings, and on the other side of the road, there is a view of Amur, the workers' housing area of Tampere. Restaurant Heinätori, the former Vaakahuone from 1914, is right next to me. It weighed hay loads and fed the horses which were used when the marketplace served the residents of the city of Tampere.

There are a couple of Nysses, i.e. buses from the city of Tampere. I stop the car. I get out of the car. From there, my co-worker arrives on foot. We hug just as is our custom at Team Academy. He lifts his backpack into the trunk and chooses the back seat. We exchange a few words and questions about the weekend. He has not been sleeping well. The coronavirus worries me. We get going. Our morning meeting starts at nine o'clock in Jyväskylä, Central Finland. The rising rays of the sun make the late winter landscape very beautiful. On the way, we discuss what the coronavirus means to us.

We arrive in Jyväskylä, known as the Athens of Finland. We have offices in the organisation Crazy Towns in Jyväskylä and Tampere. Crazy Town is a communal work community of the new era. The premises are owned by a private company founded by Mr. Mikko Markkanen. Mikko is a graduate of the Jyväskylä University of Applied Sciences Team Academy. Each individual company has its own workspace at Crazy Town locations, which also include shared meeting rooms, a coffee station, a stage and spaces for quiet work for shared use. Crazy Town in Jyväskylä is home to about 100 companies that are looking for strength from each other. We usually have our morning of dialogue meeting on Monday mornings either in Jyväskylä or Tampere.

We went into Crazy Town which is conveniently located on the high street right in the centre of Jyväskylä. The premises were formerly a large department store. I am always thrilled when I arrive here. The space has the elements of a creative space. There are inspiring and decorated workspaces such as Watercolour, Forest, Oasis and Man Cave. The entrance opens to the common coffee and working areas. There is a stage at the back. On the right is the stretching and gymnastics room. We have been reserved a space called Carnival. It has a creative and colourful atmosphere in accordance with the space reservation system. Especially this morning, we need just such an environment for our gathering.

We start the morning meeting on 16th of March 2020 at nine o'clock with a check-in, i.e. check-in is where we ask how everyone is doing. We will go through the tour for everyone, although briefly this time due to the peculiar situation. Everyone opens up a little about their own weekend, tells something about the events of the previous week, reviews a movie they have watched or a book they have read. Everyone is weighed down by today's news about the emergency law, which will enter into force in the evening. What does this mean for us? The Finnish government declares a state of emergency in Finland in the evening of the same day. Almost all face-to-face encounters must be stopped. Our company's operations are based on on-site coaching in Agritourism companies. This means the end of our activities if we do not rethink our practices and come up with something new. We decided to team up even more strongly and come up with new ideas.

We end our morning meeting and have lunch. In the afternoon, we have in Tampere a few separate meetings. Around three o'clock, we leave by car to home. I arrive back at Pyynikintori after five. I have spent ten hours on what was scheduled as a two-and-a-half-hour meeting. In retrospect, this kind of travel and use of time is a real waste of man's most important resource, namely time. Nowadays, we hold a two-and-a-half-hour meeting every Monday remotely. In addition, we have a day-long meeting once a month face-to-face at The Morva Inn, located roughly halfway between Tampere and Jyväskylä.

Change in mental patterns

The Finnish government had therefore declared a state of emergency in Finland due to the coronavirus. In practice, our entire net sales were wiped out with this decision. The winter had gone reasonably well, and we had agreed to start several long face-to-face training sessions for the end of the spring. This meant that our liquidity position was suddenly quite weak. I suggested that we try remote services. By deciding to invest the rest of our money in efficient remote systems, we would need to learn how this could be possible.

The group joined in. The idea of effective remote team coaching was completely absurd. Our mindset was that there was no way to do team coaching remotely. On top of that, we had one customer who insisted that the coaching be held the following week. This gave us an internal slogan: The Customer Relationships Act is stronger than the Emergency

Powers Act. We had no choice. We decided to invest in an efficient digital platform for dialogue, namely Howspace, and an efficient remote program, namely Zoom[2]. Business Finland opened the state financial support packages quickly. We applied for support for the development of operations during the same week. The decision was made quickly. Business Finland helped us save the company from financial ruin.

The only challenge was not holding the coaching sessions remotely. We believe in slow learning. We organise both one-day and three-day coaching. We have built six-month and one-and-a-half-year processes from them. According to remote experts, a fifteen-minute break should be taken every 45 minutes, and a few hours would be the maximum time for online teaching. We set out to try out the first team coaching in two three-hour segments. One of our most experienced team coaches bravely passed this test. We were in a hurry. The participants were satisfied, but we were not. The impact threatened to be too light. Team coaches must be able to create a safe and confidential learning environment. How on earth could we do it online and remotely?

We decided to boldly continue experimenting. We founded a Howspace[1] digital home base for team coaches, to which we invited the most enthusiastic members of the team coach network. As many as 50 enthusiastic people joined in. We believed that the same things can be done online as in real life. We started to hold dialogue sessions with team coaches remotely and built a learning process for ourselves. We gradually lengthened the online dialogue sessions, i.e. team coaching. At first, two whole days and finally as many as three. Now we work very much remotely, in the same way as in face-to-face coaching. We also developed a hybrid model, which means that some can be remote, and some can be present organically. It requires a good 360° camera, i.e. an owl (Owl Pro®), active updating of images on the digital platform and consideration of all participants.

We decided not to postpone any more coaching session. From then on, we carried out all coaching remotely, throughout the coronavirus period. When the new normal came, we held some of the coaching sessions remotely and some as hybrids. When our coaching process lasted two days, we were online for 48 hours. We and our customers have learned to conduct dialogue remotely really quite well. The biggest challenge is the disruption of remote work at home. Some learners have arranged to stay at home in peace for two days. Personally, I am in a convenient position to have an office at home. The design of one's own work and everyday life play a key role in this. Remote workers also have very different attitudes towards digital presence. I remember a case where a person had gone to look at a new cottage and a present on the phone while driving. The other person was alone at home with three children and pets. When the children came

[1] Howspace is a digital and dialogical learning platform. More information www.how space.com

[2] Zoom is an advanced remote program in which the use of video and sound as well as small group work are easy. More information www.zoom.us.

home from school, the pets were very much suffering, on the verge of freezing in the subzero temperatures and the internet connection was constantly being interrupted. The concentration of the learner was very weak. Another person went to their own cottage by themselves during the day before in time for the following day, arranged all the necessities, food, drinks, etc. and said after the coaching that this coaching is better remote than live. According to this person, the only obstacle was their own vivid imagination. We still have a lot to learn about combining home conditions and remote work.

Meaningfulness as drivers of working life

Thank you, corona, thank you. You forced us to work remotely, and we had to combine work and home. This change is about to start a new phase in the reform of working life. The value of traditional branches decreases significantly. Knowledge work will move to homes and communal workspaces that have been only occasionally used. Knowledge workers will work independently of time and place. The change is demanding from the point of view of management and employees.

A management that operates according to old-fashioned or principles of Taylorism cannot determine a suitable way of learning. The power to manage work must be handed over to employees, especially teams, not individuals. Work communities must become community driven. There is no mass of self-management. Learning in work communities and a culture of team learning are essential. Our work culture is changing. A team is not only a tool for organisation, but also for learning, growth, and development.

The new team-learning culture enables the realisation of human meaningfulness, basic psychological needs, i.e. autonomy, community and personal mastery. Management must be able to create psychological safety in the work community. And yes, autonomy means that the knowledge worker, that is to say the teacher, can decide on their own working hours and their own use of time. This is exactly what we have been doing since spring 2020. Everyone sets their own working hours. We have a morning meeting of dialogue every week on Monday. I call all the experts in our company every week and ask if there is a need for management services. I am happy when I get a call or an email asking for assistance with something.

The work community must have common rules that the work community together agree on – not the principal or the manager.

The knowledge worker can then express themselves and develop into the best version of themselves. The focus of the new work community is on the customer, not the manager. Customer thinking is not only the privilege of business experts and managers, but also of teachers and principals. The thinking of managers is changing: the customer is number one. A pupil, prisoner, citizen or elderly person are customers of the service provider. This requires defining one's own customer relationships and continuous work with customers.

In the books published in the 1980s by Tom Peters, he achieves an excellent task of highlighting the idea of an itinerant leader. A leader must learn from customers and their peers. Some time ago, a leading media house called Helsingin Sanomat filmed a Swedish train company's overnight train journey from Stockholm to Berlin. The train connection had just been opened. There was a food station on the train, which was called Secret Kapa Two. This food outlet was run by a member of the company's management. According to him, there are all kinds of adjustments in the development of a new concept, and he wanted to learn directly from customers.

Working time is an outdated concept, especially in knowledge work. In an agrarian society, work was carried out when there was work, and daylight hours made it possible to work – people rested in the dark periods. With industrialisation in the 1800s, attempts were made to act in the same way. This led to excessively long working days of 14-16 hours. The labour movement managed to fight for a reasonable working time, 40 hours a week. Since then, working hours have been a key management tool. Working time is measured to the nearest minute. It is considered a tool for measuring productivity. The trade union movement and employers agree on the framework in which the work is carried out. It is based on the notion that the employer is trying to exploit employees, and the employee is trying to slip out of work when the situation allows. This persistent conflict must end. The concept of humanity is different acquaintance. People are learning and developing. Doing away with old models requires, above all, a renewal of leadership. Change must start with employers and managers. Leaders need to break free from the control of Taylorism. Knowledge was the basis of Taylorism leadership, and it was only available to managers during industrialisation. Information has already been released and is available to everyone. Education has increased dramatically – nowadays the average knowledge worker is as educated as the manager. An equal society enables everyone to get an education and develop. What would it feel like if a team of experts determined all the grounds and goals of work based on the will of society and the needs of the customers? The leaders of the learning community would act as team coaches.

Leadership consists of three elements: managing things, leading people, and coaching.

Team coaching means that the leader utilises the team in their own leadership. The leader coaches the team, which is the basic unit of a learning organisation. An individual learns more effectively by reflecting on their own actions through a team than through the comments of leaders.

In 1993, Johannes Partanen, State Counsellor of Education, founded the Jyväskylä University of Applied Sciences (JAMK) Team Academy, which does not have actual teachers, instead it has – team coaches; there are no students – instead it has team entrepreneurs; not lessons – instead it has projects for real customers and dialogue sessions; Not specific textbooks – instead it has non-fiction books for your own needs. The leading ideas or values, mission (purpose of existence) and vision (goal of the community) of the team academy are determined by the team entrepreneurs (students) together with the team coaches (teachers).

Entrepreneurship within the work community is often a state of mind that people try to achieve. Employees who take the initiative or lead themselves get more accomplished and have intrinsic motivation.

A rather fancy English term has been coined for it, which is intrapreneurship, which is, of course, derived from the word entrepreneurship. Entrepreneurship is seen as a solution to the development of the work community, especially from the perspective of employers. Often, Johannes only offers the opportunity to work in an entrepreneurial way. Rewarding for this remains secondary. On the employee side, entrepreneurship is seen as a bogeyman in which the employee gives up their fundamental rights, and the power of the trade union movement diminishes in the workplace. We present a solution to this challenge: team entrepreneurship, which is to say joint entrepreneurship. The responsibility for the work and rewards of entrepreneurship is divided equally between the employer and the employee.

Personally, I think that an expert should answer the phone after eight o'clock in the morning, and by four o'clock in the afternoon. However, we have early risers and evening birds. I know that I can call one quite well as early as half past eight in the morning, and the other only after ten. Everyone can take holidays when they feel they need it. I make sure that everyone takes at least their statutory holidays and that working hours are recorded according to the law. Otherwise, I try to ensure that the significance of the work of the expert, i.e. personal mastery, autonomy and community, is realised. Especially during remote working, home life, hobbies and work are combined harmoniously.

A shared vision of teams is a driving force

The work community must be able to clearly define its goals and measure results within the agreed schedule. The goals should be inspiring, challenging and verbal. Each team independently defines its own goals and key results based on the goals of the work community. The model developed for defining goals and measuring results is called the Objectives and Key Results (OKR) model (source: Hämäläinen & Sora 2020). A similar approach is also used in Balanced Scorecards. In the Must Win Battles approach, the key objectives are defined more clearly, but in a leader-driven manner.

Sampo's leading thoughts

The following leading ideas of Sampo Vocational College in Finland, i.e. vision, mission and values are a useful read. In my opinion, they are profound, teacher-oriented and meet the elements of a shared vision, which I will return to later.

- Through dialogue, Sampo Vocational College in Lappeenranta, Finland has defined its shared vision: "Sampo of limitless learning – a sustainable future through co-operation."

- Sampo's mission is: "We build competence, well-being and vitality".

- Sampo's values are: "For people, the joy of learning, trust and courage".

- The focus is on people, hope and learning together. Based on these, Sampo has defined three focus areas:

  1. An evolving learning ecosystem.
  2. Learning committed and well-being personnel.
  3. Securing a sustainable future.

These guiding ideas have not only been agreed upon in the management corner room but have been accomplished through real dialogue among the entire staff. To start writing this book, I got the final inspiration from the coaching of the management team of Saimaa Vocational College in Finland, where they developed a vision, or roadmap, for building a team culture. I think the name they came up with is ingenious "Sampo of limitless learning – a sustainable future through co-operation." sufficiently informal yet rigorous. The roadmap will depict the country visually. This measure was given plenty of time, almost four years.

Sampo Vocational College is becoming a work community that learns together. Its goals will be open, time-bound, clear, qualitative and set by the community itself. There must not be too many goals. The goals can also be financial, such as reducing the team's costs. Their realisation must be monitored with key results, which are numerical. Continuous monitoring of goals and results is key. They form the team's own shared vision.

Breakfast with Peter Senge

I am an avid listener of audiobooks, mainly due to the fact that I am rather a slow reader due to a slight dyslexia issue. I participated in the Society of Learning Organisations (SoL) conference in Stockholm in 2010. I tend to exercise in different ways on my way to work. This time I was able to rent a bike from the hotel reception so I could exercise by cycling before breakfast. During my cycle I listened to Peter Senge's Fifth Discipline. I cycled for an hour and a half. After returning to my room and showering, I came to breakfast in an enthusiastic mood. I opened up to the next in the queue about my already completed morning's bike ride and about the thrilling audiobook experience. After the first burst of enthusiasm, I was surprised to find found out the next person in line whom I was talking to turned out to be no other than Peter Senge himself. I talked Peter enthusiastically about his book about the learning organisation. After getting over my sudden surprise at the coincidence, Peter asked if he could join me for breakfast. We sat at breakfast together and enjoyed almost two hours of intensive discussion about learning.

Peter Senge had visited Team Academy back in the 1990s and was immensely excited about what he saw and experienced. He had followed the development of the Team Academy through Mondragon's Team Academy and sent congratulatory videos to the Team Academy's birthday parties, among other things. From this discussion, I remembered the term shared vision, which is one of the building blocks of a learning organisation. Peter Senge defines the elements of a learning organisation in the book as follows: personal mastery, mindsets, shared vision, team learning, and systems thinking.

Work communities usually define the leading ideas (vision, mission, values) in the management corner room and the board then decides on them.

According to Peter Senge, a shared vision answers the question: What do we want to create? Work communities must engage in long-term and correct dialogue to ensure that the vision is genuinely shared. I have followed the transformation of the Finnish LocalTapiola (LähiTapiola) insurance company into a Lifelong Security company. I remember well the surprise of a management representative in one of the training sessions: "This three-year strategy period is already coming to an end, but only now are our experts beginning to understand what our vision is and where we are going."

Over the next three-year period, LocalTapiola's vision is to grow into a lifelong security company. The vision began to become a shared vision through dialogue. Lifelong security is on the agenda in all speeches, and it clearly inspires LocalTapiola residents. LocalTapiola's values are profound: courage, enthusiasm, passion and benevolence. The lifeguards of the entire company participated in the value process. There was a lot of discussion about benevolence in particular, and dialogue showed its power: benevolence became an essential value. Rarely in my career have I encountered such an inspiring shared vision in a large company. Nokia's vision from the 1990s, Connecting People, was on the same level, as it inspired the entire company.

I have been coaching another work community where the decision to switch to the team model was announced suddenly out of the blue. The leader presented me with a presentation based on war metaphors and told me that he would declare a team model war the very next day. At the same time, we agreed on coaching co-operation. In that war, there was some loss of personnel, as no one had been trained for teamwork. Even though the change itself happened immediately on paper, it took the organisation a couple of years to adopt and put the team model into practice. There are many different paths to a good goal. Learning is slower than a fast pace.

A shared vision realises a combination of an emerging strategy and the desired strategy. Henry Mittsberg, a philosopher of strategy, has pondered how strategy actually takes shape. Management plans the vision and strategy, after which these are discussed with the workforce. Part of the vision is rejected, and part of the vision becomes a shared vision. Figure 2 describes a company's strategic planning and its implementation. It is from Mintsberg in (1994), from the book The Rise and Fall of Strategic Planning. A shared vision is important if the work community wants to become a team learner. Creating a shared vision requires genuine dialogue and perseverance.

Figure 2. The development of a shared vision
(adapted from Mintsberg 1994).

Putting the learner at the centre of actual learning

The classroom originated in the workroom of a sewing machine factory in the 1800s. Sewing machines were removed an lo and behold, the classroom was ready. Children learned discipline and obedience. The role of the teacher was patron-like. When parents and adults went to work in factories, children were desired to be somewhere out of the way, to learn working life skills. When I started studying at university in Otaniemi, Finland, in the 1980s, there had been no change. In the large Aalto Hall, several hundred students listened to a lecture on mathematics. The charisma of the lecturer had withered so much in 150 years that his duties had been given to a doctoral researcher who was an introvert. He muttered and drew something completely incomprehensible on the drawing projector. While he was drawing on the slide, he accidentally erased some of his drawings with his sleeve. At the end, I got my worst grade in the mathematics course in the university at Otaniemi, even though my mathematics number was 10 throughout upper secondary school and I wrote the best grade Laudatur in the school from the matriculation examination.

The management of educational institutions has developed more slowly than in business life. Unfortunately, the impact of the coronavirus on the world of education has not been positive. Teaching moved flexibly to remote learning, but teacher-centredness increased. It increased the inequality of pupils and reduced the sense of community. There are certainly good remote teaching lessons, but as mass lectures have moved to remote implementation, there are also many bad ones, especially in universities that are lagging behind in pedagogy. Universities have a strong professorial and science-centred approach, and the research and development of pedagogy belong only to the Department of Education. A professor is not expected to have any teaching skills, unlike those working in all educational institutions, from kindergarten to upper secondary school and vocational college. Even as a name, education emphasises the centrality of the teacher and the system. Learning science would be a better name.

One of the reasons for poor remote learning is poor software. For cost reasons, many places use engineering-inspired MS Teams software, because MS Teams comes with Microsoft software. Learning interaction is supported by the use of images, an easy-to-use connection and easy division of participants into small groups. These are not included in the MS Teams security areas. MS Teams is similar to the Nokia Communicator mobile phone from 2005. Instead, Zoom offers these features needed for learning, it's like the iPhone smartphone from 2023. However, MS Teams continues to evolve. Meetings go well with MS Teams, but the use of this platform for effective dialogue is very rigid. One option is digital platforms where it is possible to engage in dialogue, share learning materials and make learning communal during and, above all, between encounters or lectures. Most learning platforms are suitable for storing information, not for dialogue effectiveness. The Howspace learning platform is just like the aforementioned iPhone only from 2024.

One university researcher commented that reforming the world of education is as slow as moving a cemetery. In addition to technical and financial challenges, the relocation of the cemetery involves significant value conflicts based on worldviews, or the benefits achieved. Changing the world of education is a similar thing. The most important aspect, i.e. the learner, student or pupil themselves, is easily left in a secondary role. Working life, parents, municipal budget, state policy and school buildings play a more important role.

Finland is a pioneering country in learning. Finland is helped by an equal society where teachers are generally competent and well educated. The work of teachers is highly appreciated. Still, we are only at the beginning of the reform of learning. The vast majority are still wondering whether learning should be reformed. The situation is best in basic education and vocational colleges, whereas at university level, we are still relying on innovators, which means that a few enthusiastic experimenters are trying to reform pedagogy.

Renewing learning requires long-term patience. Peter Senge superbly described the process of change in systems thinking in his book The Dance of Change (1999). See Figure 3. Change starts with the community. The first step is to create an inspiring atmosphere in the community (Y2) and a willingness to commit. In the works of Eric Ries (2011) and John Kotter (1996/2009), change in the community begins with experiments and small pilots. It is worth investing so much in the first experiments that enthusiasm spreads and the people in the work community commit. Through this, changes begin to take place in the prevailing culture. Through delays in the individual's circle (Y1), the development of abilities and personal results begin. It is only in the outermost circle of results (Y3) that new practices and sustainable results are created. This change will take its time.

According to my own experience, a change in an educational institution or work community takes at least 3-5 years before the change is rooted and credibility is achieved. After the establishment of the Team Academy and Proakademia, both units achieved such convincing results after five years that they could no longer be undone. The problem is usually the lack of courage of management. Management can notice that team learning achieves results and publicity. It is really quite pitiful to watch from the sidelines if management does not comprehend the effectiveness of team learning. I have heard the following results and comments:

- Employment at vocational schools increased from 50 per cent to as much as 75 per cent, and feedback from working life was excellent.

- At best, the entrepreneurship rate has risen by 30-50 per cent and all graduates have found work (achieved in vocational schools and universities of applied sciences).

- Experienced pedagogical developer: "I have seen a lot of different courses, methods and magic tricks in my life to improve basic education, but the sense of community and co-guidance created by team learning is the only thing that brings about lasting positive changes."

- The overall index of the educational institution's personnel survey increased from 3.66 to 4.03 and rose to be the best of the educational consortium in three years.

More than fifty theses have been written on team learning: at lower and higher academic levels, master's theses, scientific articles and some doctoral dissertations. A list of these can be found on the Team Academy website. I have failed to come across any negative research on the benefits of collaborative learning. Dr. Elinor Vettraino and her team in England were inspired to compile scientific articles on team learning from the Team Academy network into a series of four books. The respected publisher Routledge published the first book in late 2021 and the last in March 2022. There were thirty-five articles, of which the author of this book participated in one.

.

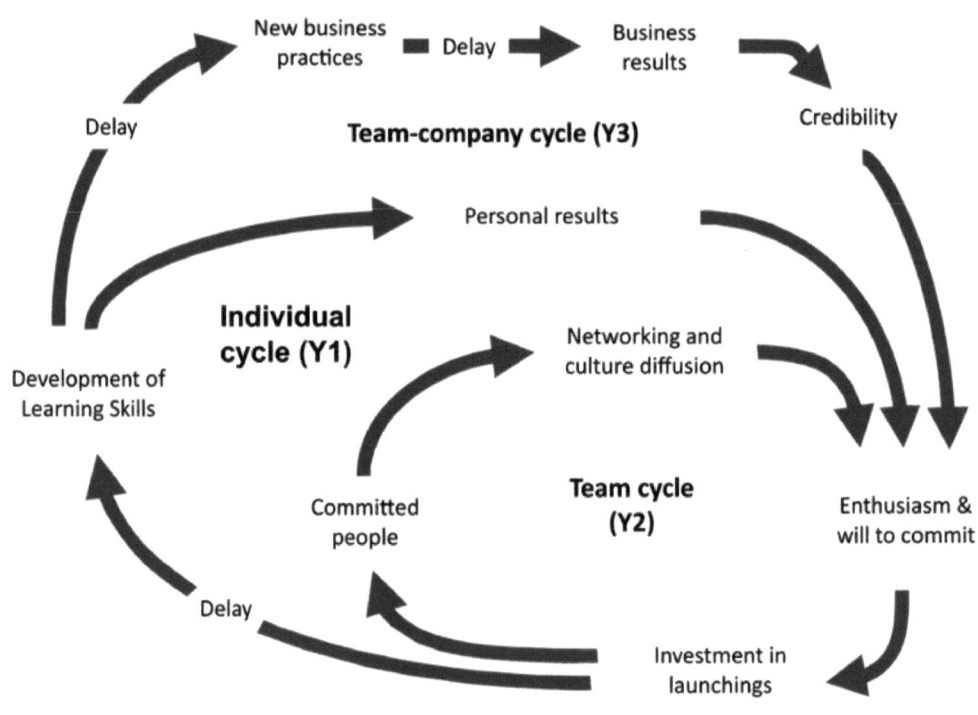

Figure 3. The Circles of Learning (Senge, 1999).

3. Why is the team being built?

Co-operation is a person's area of strength

Organisations dream of self-managing employees. I question this idea, because human strength lies in co-operation. Organisations must be co-directed, i.e. team learning. Henrik von Wright is one of Finland's greatest philosophers. His logical thinking includes non-thinking. Imagine there would be no teams in the work community, and they would not be wanted in the workplace. The work community would work in such a way that everyone would only do their own work, which would be so clearly defined and directed from above so that co-operation is not required. However, Henry Ford's car factory was already so developed that co-operation was indeed required. So, this option can be ruled out. The next chance between people is for loose co-operation in the group. What separates a group from a team is a commitment to a goal. If a group has a shared vision, it is a team. In other words, the work community would work as groups that are aware of each other but would not want to achieve the same goal. The group achieves a flimsy apparent effect, i.e. the actual productivity of the group is weak. This type of group organisation was probably the Taylorism management philosophy of Henry Ford's car factory. Precise instructions, discipline and an incentive bonus guide the work community forward.

Many work communities are fixed in a group organisation, even though the operating units are called teams. This is a problem. I met the HR director of a unit of a stock exchange listed company, who had to meet secretly with his own group, as working hours were not allowed to be used for unnecessary meetings. However, he talked about a team. Team is a much nicer term than group, leading to the term team being widely misused. A group is a group of people whose members are aware of their own membership, the membership of others, and a common mission. The group is not committed to completing the task together. If a team is without a shared vision, it is correctly called a group. A group becomes a team when the team members commit to completing the task of the team. The team has a shared vision. What separates a team from a group is a common goal, rules of the game and a common time to meet. Organisations should be honest with themselves and talk about a group organisation instead of a team organisation.

From fear to courage – from leader or expert to team coach

Change is usually a fearful thing. One of Peter Senge's principles of a learning organisation is mental models. The organisation develops a common way of thinking, i.e. a common belief system. People in an organisation in a particular sector have a similar view of the activities in their own area. This thinking is what I refer to as the mindset.

In the learning organisation you have to break learned mental patterns and create new ones. Supervisors are afraid to delegate power, and experts are afraid to take responsibility. Traditionally, senior managers have become accustomed to controlling their actions, and team members have learned to take instructions.

In coaching leadership, the supervisor must learn to create safety and ask encouraging and insightful questions. Team members must learn a new way of thinking, where each project team takes care of things independently and within an agreed framework. Indicators that are known to everyone, agreed upon and visualised are the key to achieving success. When the matter is complete, it is considered in the learning team and learned collectively.

Team thinking was introduced in many organisations in the 1990s, when Peter Senge and many other team writers became enthusiastic. In many cases, however, these teams were just tools of organisation, i.e. groups, and not real teams. According to Senge, the team is first and foremost a tool for learning, not for organisation.

In handing over power to learners, the teacher or leader relinquishes control. In this case, the possibility of mistakes must also be accepted. A mistake is always an opportunity to learn from.

Many good books have been written about this, such as Awesome Mistake (Sutinen & Kuitunen 2018). According to my own empirical observations, leaders, teachers, and experts make mistakes alike. The greater the power, the greater the mistake and the more likely it is to be swept under the carpet. It often happens that an action is called a mistake even though it has not yet been tested on a real customer.

I myself studied the leadership of millennials more than ten years ago in a local development agency funded leader project. At that time, I built a peer leadership model, where power is shared equally with the leader/expert and the teacher/learner. In peer leadership, it is essential to be more than an acquaintance, i.e. to know the other party at a sufficient level. It is important to be less than a friend, i.e. not to favour a team member as a friend too much. The best thing is to be a friend, more than an acquaintance, but less than a friend. The friends know each other reasonably well but are able to make independent decisions. I based the model of peer leadership on the Japanese samurai philosophy, the book Earth, Water, Fire, Wind and Emptiness (1654) written by Miyamoyo Mushashi. In the first ground phase, both parties are able to lead themselves. In the second water phase, a shared vision is defined. In the third fire phase, the value of bringing energy and giving space in doing is understood. In the fourth wind phase, something new is brought to your own industry. The highest form of leadership is emptiness, i.e. conscious presence – we only have this moment, and we must seize it.

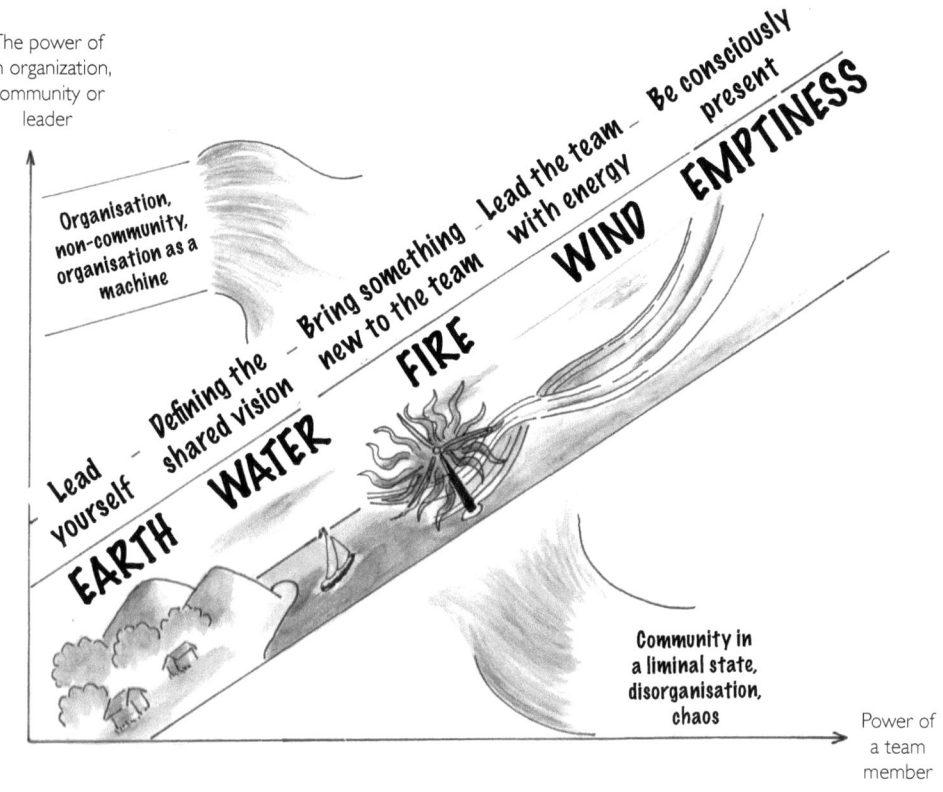

The power of an organization, community or leader

Organisation, non-community, organisation as a machine

EARTH — Lead yourself

WATER — Defining the shared vision

FIRE — Bring something new to the team

WIND — Lead the team with energy

EMPTINESS — Be consciously present

Community in a liminal state, disorganisation, chaos

Power of a team member

Figure 4. The steps of peer leadership.

Into a work community that learns together

The building blocks of team-learning culture are a learning team, a project team, time, vision, rules, a team coach, encouragement, acceptance of different paces, competence and a persistent sense of purpose.

How do you build one? Peter Senge raised the concept of a learning organisation in his book The Fifth Discipline (1991). A learning organisation consists of five elements: systems thinking, personal, mastery, mindsets, shared vision, and team learning. The organisation and its members should recognise their own actions as part of a larger whole and their interdependencies as part of the system. Every member of a learning organisation should have the opportunity to develop themselves and be at their best in the work community, i.e. to realise their personal mastery. A learning organisation engages in a dialogue about the belief systems or mindsets related to its own company, market, technology and competitors. A shared vision means the goal of the entire organisation: the members of the organisation do not go towards the goal because of a command, but on the basis of their own desire and passion. Team learning begins with dialogue, i.e. the ability to think together, in which team members learn about themselves and each other in the team. Team entrepreneurship, i.e. entrepreneurship together, is central to the Team Academy model. Team entrepreneurship could be the sixth building block of a learning organisation. Perhaps this is a critical element in building a learning work community.

Building a learning organisation requires dismantling old structures and creating new ones. It requires:

1. Division into learning teams and smaller project teams belonging to them.
2. Joint dialogue time.
3. A common goal (shared vision).
4. Common rules and a team agreement.
5. Team Coach.
6. Reading related to one's own learning.
7. Learning by doing.

Learning team and project team

Combining learning and the organisation of teams requires a new structure. A learning team is a team comprising of a maximum of around 25 people. It is a suitable team for sharing learning and taking care of a larger entity. In addition to this, from the point of view of the actual management of things, i.e. organisation, the team must be divided into smaller project teams of about 2-7 people. Project teams take care of the tasks of the team and its goals. You can combine team learning and organisation in this way. Above all, a team is a tool for learning, not just for organisation. The lessons learned from the project teams must be shared in the learning team. Building a team takes time, because trust must be built between team members. Trust is not created easily. In order for a learning team to be a tool for learning, its maximum size can be around 25 people. This is because dialogue in a larger team becomes slow. Another factor limiting the size is the slowdown in building trust as the team size grows. Team members are unable to familiarise with each other as well in a larger team.

The project team and the learning team require leadership to be built within the team. They should have a team leader, which is different from a team coach. The team leader can be changed from time to time. The best leadership is created when the teams themselves choose the team leaders. The learning team can also have a management team. Gatherings should be prepared. In the beginning, the team coach can set an example, but it is extremely important that the team itself takes responsibility for the meetings and their preparation.

This is central to team learning in schools. In other words, there is a learning team, i.e. a class from which project teams are formed. In a basic education school, teachers in a parallel class placed forty second-grade pupils in the same group. They started coaching teams instead of just traditional teaching. Two classes were divided into two groups of about five pupils, each of whom had their own distinctive colour. There were not many team leaders in these, but the "laundry persons" were responsible for the day's small tasks, such as distributing supplies to their own group. For the pupils, the laundry shift played an important role. The nest groups will remain the same throughout the six weeks period and new groups and team leaders will be changed for every six weeks. Before the change, it felt like there were a few slightly lonelier people in the class, who might not have the motivation to go to school, and there was concern about them. Now that they have switched to co-teaching and nest groups, they have made new friends and their motivation for school has increased. The sense of community and joy at school have strengthened and returned, it is very important, in addition to learning, that the pupils enjoy themselves and experience a sense of community. From the teachers' point of view, the best thing is the lightening of their own workload and increased flexibility.

PROJECT TEAM

- Size: 2-7 people per case.
- Task: Implementation of (customer) projects. Everyone has their own role, and the project has its own goals.
- Members: Members of a learning team, can also be members outside another team or community.
- Time span: the team is together for the duration of the project.
- Main focus: Customer relationships, operations, application of theory in practice.

TEAM COACH

Participates in the learning team training, listening, reflection, asking questions, sparring, sometimes giving advice and feedback.

Team coach can be also the leader of the learning team or there can be a separate team leader or captain.

LEARNING TEAM

- Size 15-25 people
- Task: regular training and sharing experiences and lessons learned from the projects. The team has jointly created rules, values and goals
- Members: This is made up of community members
- Time span: The ideal is permanence, at best, the team is together for years.
- Main focus: Learning, reflection, sharing knowledge in the community, building mutual trust

Figure 5. Learning team, project team and team coach.

The structure of the learning team and an ice hockey team is very similar. The team itself has about 25 members, who are divided into smaller chains of five players. Each chain, or project team, has its own task. Usually, the main task of the 1st and 2nd lines is to score the winning goals. The task of the 3rd and 4th lines is to defend and take energy from the opponent. In addition to this, there are separate lines for power play and shorthanded play, i.e. project teams.

The entire team has a captain (the team leader of the learning team) and vice-captains, who form the learning team, i.e. the leadership of the team. In addition to this, each line has its own leading players.

I have listened on several occasions to Mr. Erkka Westerlund, who is the former Finnish National Men's Ice Hockey Team Head Coach and coach of national ice-hockey league teams, and we have even had some professional collaboration. Erkka has developed his own coaching style, which he calls people-oriented as opposed to coach-oriented. Erkka's speeches and his book highlight the hard work of coaches in selecting the team:

> "There are not as many top players in Finland as with other countries. The difference must be compensated for by co-operation between the players – namely team play."

Erkka wanted healthy and strong players in the team who were ready to work together. The turning point in his career was the Turin Olympics, where the Finnish national team did not have a large enough gathering space for the entire team. This led to line-specific coaching, where each line took responsibility for its own game. Finland won an amazing Olympic silver medal. Erkka's winning quotation is:

> "Learning is more important than winning."

Another thing that comes up in Erkka's stories and book is the coach's preparation and the selection of players. In working life, the dynamics of the team are much less considered. I admit that the national ice hockey team is a very different team than the normal team at work. Often the leader of the work community or the team coach has no or small opportunities to influence the composition of their own team. But the position of employees in different project teams or their tasks can always be influenced by the manager. The leader or team coach has a big impact on the atmosphere of the team. This is an especially crucial factor in building a team.

I vividly remember when I once visited a factory manager who had just started in his role. He told about the difficult situation at the factory. In addition to him, his team had included three managers: Production Manager, Maintenance Manager and the Development Manager. The factory had made a loss. The problems were poor co-operation between production and maintenance, as well as the lack of a clear goal. The Development Director dreamed of a large investment that would sweep all the current problems under the carpet. The new Factory Manager was of the opinion that it would be better to first get the current operations into a state of affairs before making investments. The Factory Manager came up with a radical solution: he relieved the Development Director of his position. Then he swapped the positions of Production Manager and Maintenance Manager. Co-operation between production and maintenance began to work excellently. The factory also began to make small repairs on a continuous basis that saw the operation turn to profitability.

Time

For the group to become a learning team, enough time must be reserved for its gathering and dialogue. The team must have circular and rectangular meetings.

By circular meeting, I mean dialogic events. A dialogical event or session is a get together in an empty space where there is no official agenda. There are three phases to this get together event. Login, which we refer to as check-in. This is followed by the discussion of the theme or themes. The themes can be brought up at the check-in phase or they have been agreed upon in advance. The session ends by checking out. In good dialogical events, trust is at such a high level that the participants dare to talk about their own true emotional state. In some check-in situations, personal reasons such as sadness or joy are experienced. Once the participant has talked about them, they are able to free themselves into a genuine dialogue and the other participants understand the person's emotional state. When trust is high enough, this initial stage can take up to hours. I vividly remember a dialogical event of less than fifteen people, the total duration of which was four hours. Check-in took three hours. After that, we started checking out.

In actual team discussions, i.e. the dialogue session, the content issues arise, all the things that need to be collectively decided. It is equally important that each team member can ask for help, support and suggestions for solutions for themselves. The dialogic session also ends with a final discussion, i.e. a check-out. In this, everyone evaluates the success of the session, reflects on their own learning, next actions and plans.

The duration of the dialogue training is at least two hours, preferably four. Dialogue sessions should take place at least once every two weeks – I recommend weekly. In addition, time should be reserved for rectangular encounters between the learning team or project teams (or parts of them). During these meetings, members have to agree on the matters to be taken care of and make appropriate decisions. Co-operation between the team leaders of the project teams is also key. Team leaders must agree with each other on the activities of the teams. They agree on what kind of project teams the team needs and define their core task.

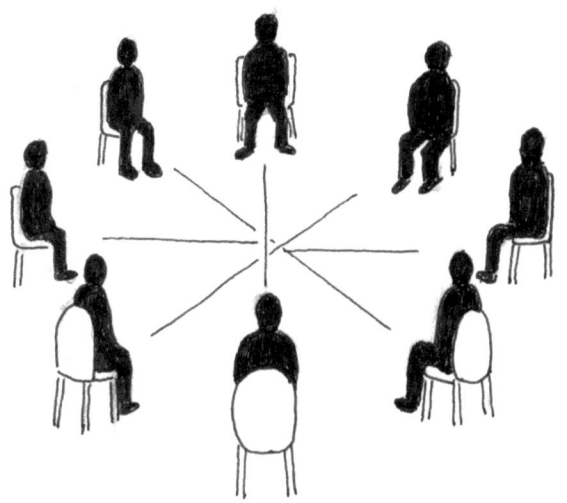

CIRCLE OF DIALOGUE SESSION

Primarily for learning teams

People in the lead role

Check-in > dialogue on the theme > check-out

RECTANGULAR MEETING

Primarily for project teams

Issues and decisions are the main roles

Check-in > presentation of the issue or issues and Decision > check-out

Figure 6. Circle session and rectangular meeting

Teams can have many kinds of get togethers. Dialogue circle sessions in which people, dialogue and learning are the main roles. Dialogue circle sessions are mainly for learning teams. Rectangular meetings aimed at decision-making focus on issues and decision-making. Rectangular meetings are mainly for project teams. One leader quite wisely said, "I try to maximise the dialogue sessions, because the wisdom is in the people and in their thoughts." The team coach or team leader must take crystallisation and decision-making into account during dialogue sessions. Dialogue should lead to experimentation and learning by doing, preferably directly with the customer. These experiments and actions become content for the next dialogue session events.

Shared Vision

A common goal must be developed for the learning team, i.e. a shared vision. A good goal cannot only be a vision agreed upon and implemented by the management, but the vision must arise from the team members. The leader may have an idea of a vision that is subordinated to a dialogue with the entire team. The vision of the management, personnel and owners is formed into a single shared vision, i.e. a common direction. A shared vision is a genuine vision of the organisation, which is not a one-way order given by the management. The role of the personnel in creating a shared vision is central. The role of the management is to function as a coach for the entire organisation. Recording and visualising a common vision is very important. Recording a shared vision in a team agreement is highly recommended. In fact, a shared vision is the core of a team agreement: it is a shared roadmap for the development and goals of the team.

Even though the team can know their own numerical targets with relative precision, I recommend presenting it in verbal and/or visual form. I have seen multi-page instructions from management on team agreements that dampen enthusiasm for a shared vision. I vividly remember the legendary ice hockey coach Risto Dufva, of a national ice hockey league team, telling me that there cannot be a more boring objective for a team than 78 points in the regular season. This amount is likely to guarantee first place in the regular season and a place in the playoffs. Instead, the team thought up a verbal goal themselves, which had to be fulfilled in every action of each player, every moment. This verbal goal was easy to compare to every action of each player on the field.

Rules of the game

The teams must agree on common ground rules. They should be strict enough to enable the team's common goal to be achieved. On the other hand, the rules of the game must be sufficiently loose. They must allow the personal significance of the team members to take shape: autonomy, personal mastery, doing good and the development of a sense of community. The basic principles of dialogue form a good basis for common rules: voicing, respecting, listening and suspending. If the teamwork thinks through fun, then rules of the game are the team's boundaries. It is a good idea to solidify and visually confirm the rules of the game by writing them down in a joint and visual team agreement. A team agreement creates a culture of team learning.

> *The team coach should transfer as much responsibility as possible to the team, and let the team make its own mistakes. The team's rules are an area where he must be careful.*

If a culture that weakens atmosphere is created in the team, then it is difficult to remedy it. I, myself, once messed with the rules of the team. There were a few people in the team, one in particular, who was very skilled at being hostile. They formed a small but sharp opposition to the team and really backed each other up with effect. This person of negative influence, implied that he supported a person or an act in the team but made the whole activity questionable and ridiculed it. Due to my natural kind nature, I did not know how to effectively intervene in this situation. I should have been assertive to stop this type of behaviour from the team. This naturally weakened the performance and spirit of the entire team. The rules of the team form the backbone of the team.

Team Agreement

The team agreement made by the team, and the team's own rules, play key roles in the team's development. The team agreement is drawn up for a longer period of time: the direction, with what conditions, resources, capabilities and schedule. The team's rules of the game agree on the team's code of conduct, schedule, commitment, support from a friend or going from behind. In ideal circumstances, these would have been agreed in the same written agreement, but the rules of the team are often unwritten, a mental model that the team thinks collectively. This can be called the team paradigm, i.e. the team's shared understanding of the team's rules. The team paradigm can be different in each team member's own mind if there has not been enough dialogue about the common rules. The team coach's work is naturally made much easier by writing down both of these in the form of a contract or a visual drawing that everyone signs.

I remember one team of team entrepreneurs (= students) agreeing on a late arrival fine of 100 euros to be imposed on anyone turning up late for the team's dialogue training. I think this is quite excessive, though. However, team discipline and respect for other team members increased significantly. The team took many development steps towards a top team. I remember thinking that the hourly rate of one normal meeting of my own operating unit's team during my Valmet-era was about the same as the hourly rate of a medium-sized paper machine operating time, i.e. at least 5000 euros. Being late always results in lost efficiency, so compared to this amount, a fine of 100 euros was reasonable. However, it is noted that not all working time efficiency can be measured and valued in this way alone.

The most important thing about a team agreement is that it is informal and looks like the team. In my opinion, the team agreement and the rules of the team should have the following elements:

1. Shared vision – The direction of the team
2. Clear purpose – Why the team exists
3. Desire to work with others, i.e. meetings (time, rhythm)
4. Courage to question constructively
5. Clear rules on the structure of the team, i.e. project teams and the learning team
6. Respect and encouragement of others
7. Desire to learn and help others learn
8. Trust and openness
9. Reporting, tolerating and resolving errors
10. Is informal and has risen from the team

Our own team signed a team agreement for the spring of 2021. We emphasised the role of each team member, the atmosphere, the way they work through projects, everyone's own learning agreement, the values and the principles. We considered it important to meet regularly. We wanted to keep up the good energy by noting the achievements. Our shared vision was "rushing into the summer". We succeeded.

Team Coach

I cannot imagine a sports team without a coach. How could a company operate without a CEO, especially if he or she did not coach experts in addition to his or her own work? A team needs a captain, i.e. a leader and a coach. A team coach or coaching leader forms the basis for building a team. The team coach monitors the development of the team and patiently builds the team's own culture. As a rule, the team coach functions through a coaching approach. I touch more on the role of a team coach in the following chapter.

Learning agreement – a plan for your own life

In my mind, I have been thinking about the plan of my own life. I noticed that it can also be planned in writing when I came to the Team Academy of the Jyväskylä University of Applied Sciences. There I got two teams to coach. I was a team coach and got into the team championships. There I came across a learning contract that I had to make all by myself. In his book The Wisdom of Strategic Learning (1994), Ian Cunnigham describes the learning contract and shows its importance in improving learning outcomes throughout the organisation. A learning contract is a plan for the development of one's own competence. It helps to perceive one's own goals and understand what kind of learning tools are necessary to use in order to achieve one's own goals. The format of the learning contract is simple: it consists of five open-ended questions. Typically, it is drawn up for a time span of six months or a year, although it is possible to draw it up for a longer period. The contract is made with the person and the organisation they represent. It is important to share it with your own work community. In this case, co-workers and supervisors can help achieve goals.

I made my first written learning contract and realised that I wanted to be an entrepreneur. To become a factory owner to be precise. I started looking for machining shops to acquire long with a business idea. At the same time, my long-term marriage came to an end, and I wasted my energy on the furious search for entrepreneurship. I thought I knew how to coach teams. Through the crisis, I realised that I should focus on my core task. I renewed my learning contract: focus on smaller issues, and you will get a lot achieved. I focused on coaching the teams and doing my task properly. I started to get results. I made a book about peer leadership. Suddenly, I was offered the position of Managing Director of Team Academy Global Oy and a shareholding. I got to work as a brain construction manufacturer. I then found new love and remarried. I updated the learning contract to last until 2028. I started to make a visual curriculum for six months. I wrote there that I want a wonderful wife and family. I had found my new wife and moved to Pispala in Tampere, Finland, thanks to love.

In Finland, things need to be achieved by Midsummer and Christmas. The work of a brain construction factory has not always been easy. I am grateful for all the lessons I have learned in my previous positions. The most important lesson is to learn all the time. In my work, I am living my current dream, and it has a meaning: we create bold team coaches.

Reading related to personal learning

Reading creates new perspectives. Read and always. I have always enjoyed books. However, due to my dyslexia, I am a natural slow reader, so I enjoy audiobooks more. My reading has gone in waves. Sometimes I read more, sometimes less. When I look back on my own life, my development has always slowed down when I am not reading. Reading gives me new ideas and inspiration for life. I read books for an important personal need. I get inspiration and new ideas from books.

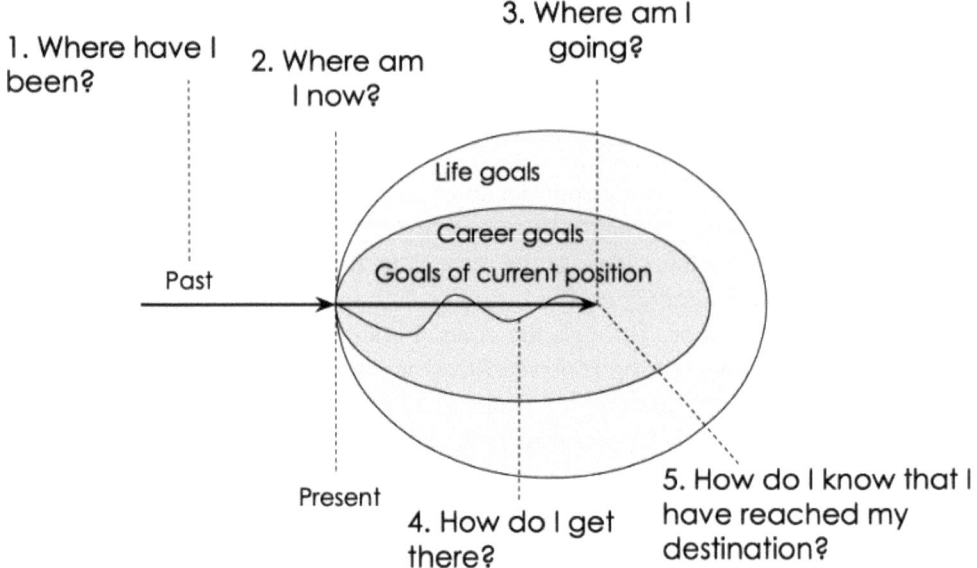

Figure 7. A plan for one's own life – a learning contract
(Ian Cunningham, 1999).

Learning by doing

I learn by doing. I am at my best when I notice that I am excellent at what I do. Sometimes I have to go to an area where I am not so proficient. Or sometimes mistakes happen that you have to admit to yourself and those involved. If you do not bring your own mistakes to light, then you will not learn from them. Reflection on learning by doing is at its best in dialogue with the team. Then you can really reflect on how good you are and how much you can still learn. If I believe I am excellent at something, then my development stops. Conversely, if I think I am bad, then my performance is not very good.

A few empirical observations and book recommendations to assist you in realising your dream

A plan will help you to help you realise your dream. Today I walked to the local antiquarian bookshop after a meeting. There I found a book called Inner Hero by the Finnish author and head of Trainers' House Jari Sarasvuo that was first published in 1996. I read it in the park the same day. Back in the autumn of 2016, I also participated in an online course by Jari Sarasvuo called "Halve the Frustration and Double the Results III". During this course, Jari Sarasvuo spoke vividly and visualised during the course: "Before long, a map will be drawn."

In the book called Aki Hintsa's The Core – Better Life, Better results by Oskari Saari who is a Finnish sports journalist, Formula 1 and ice hockey commentator, the meaning of the core, or one's own humanity, through the following three questions is described:

1. Who am I?
2. What do I want?
3. Am I in control of my own life?

The third question in particular brings new insight when someone else tends to dominate our own lives. Based on my own experiences and literature, I warmly recommend the learning agreement.

Oskari Saari also wrote a successful book called The Road to Success in which the book describes the legendary Petteri Nykky who is a highly accomplished Finnish floorball coach. Petteri Nykky's coaching philosophy for the national floorball team, and how Finland won its first gold medal and even renewed is discussed. In this book, it is described how Petteri made all the team members write their own personal goals at the national team camps. He threw himself aside in international matches and allowed the team to build its own success, supporting a true winning culture uncompromisingly.

According to Erkka Westerlund, the development of one's own self-knowledge starts with attention to oneself (reflection). In the second step, after knowing oneself, self-management becomes possible. In the third step, you can systematically develop yourself through working together, i.e. as a team. In the fourth and final step, you can develop into a coaching leader. Erkka's motto is "The big five of my life and sport" which describes the philosophical core of coaching. They are intrinsic motivation, attitude, self-confidence, responsibility and a sense of performance.

You can also learn about sports coaching through. Henrik Dettman's book The Art of Leadership, which was written by Saska Saarikoski an accomplished Finnish journalist.

The learning agreement of one's own life requires action. I think of strategy as being a verb, because strategy requires action. It requires perseverance and repetition. Many books emphasise micro-change as the elements of change.

In The Sprit of Kaizen, by Maurer and Hirschman (2012) the elements of change are nicely described: Change must be so small that it does not cost anything and it benefits the customer.

Chet Holmes (2008), as a karate master and sales guru, emphasises the importance of repetition in development. The self-help literature is very extensive. If you have a suitable state of mind, they will help you develop yourself.

In his book called Eat That Frog, Brian Tracy claims that only three percent of people have a written plan for their lives. I believe in this figure, because three percent indicates the low circulation of both Team Academy's and Ian Cunnigham's books, the latter of which is admittedly a challenging read. I am unsure where Brian Tracy derived this percentage from, though. However, the main point of the book is to complete the most difficult task right away, even if it is not very pleasant.

A similar book is The Five Second Rule (Mel Robbins 2017). The book tells the story of how Mel, the author, rose from a ragged life to prosperity with this very simple advice.

The following books are also very useful:

- James Clear's (2018) book Atomic Habits describes how to develop routines from good things.
- Danish author Svend Brinkmann's (2016) book Stay Strong – Life Without Self-Help provides spartan-style instructions for finding oneself and one's roots. Ironically, it is a self-help book that opposes self-help books.
- Personally, I fell in love with Grace Beverley's book Working hard – hardly working (2021). Grace Beverly shares the 24-year-old's self-management and entrepreneurship with great confidence while telling her own entrepreneurial story. I had switched to using iPad drawing programs, but I was inspired by this book, I then reverted back to using a paper notebook and coloured pencils again. I praised the book so much and so often in our dialogue training that the title of the book became "a book-that-can't-be-named-anymore". I have listened to this book three times.

Cultural change is a path of perseverance and determination

If an organisation thinks it is the best and its development needs are not highlighted, then the organisation will generally regress. Traditionally, work communities have a very strong culture of working alone. This can be seen starting from management teams. Often, they have a competitive spirit, leaders are competitive and want to continue to advance their careers. This leads to the fact that people easily play against each other resulting in the disappearance of real openness. These leaders tend to try and cover up their own mistakes and are ready to reveal the mistakes of others. Management Group is a good name for a collection of managers: the members are aware of each other but are not committed to a common goal. A management team, on the other hand, commits to a common goal, i.e. a shared vision.

With the help of a management team, better results can be achieved, but it takes time to construct a team. Therefore, the coaching leader must create an atmosphere of trust, which means extreme openness and acknowledgment of one's own vulnerability.

Brené Brown in her book Dare to lead (2020/2018), writes about building psychological safety. Psychological safety is central to building trust. Brené Brown effectively describes this by collecting marbles in a large glass jar. Every confidential act of a leader brings one marble to the jar. An act that inspires distrust can remove one, several, or even all of the marbles at once. When a glass jar is full of marbles, trust is high.

The job description of experts and the use of working hours are very strictly determined in a traditional work community. There is very limited time and opportunities for teamwork. I have come across work communities where the salary of an expert consists of seven different elements and the use of working hours is defined within fifteen minutes of accuracy. This type of work community is a prisoner of agreements. In a situation like this, one coaching manager instructed the work community as follows: "I try to minimise the time reserved for formal meetings and maximise informal time."

Making a cultural change is a long road that requires a goal. Change requires perseverance and determination. Continuous dialogue and learning by doing are essential. Openly highlighting the results and even unsuccessful experiments is key to learning. Building a team culture is a bold and exceptional goal. A culture of learning creates real impacts: the atmosphere in the organisation flourishes and learning outcomes improve.

Team learning is experiential learning

I arrived at the training place at precisely the same time as the trainer of the adjacent room opened their door. We greeted each other and then the trainer announced that a "coaching" would be held. I was somewhat stunned by this statement. I looked at the layout in the prepared training space with tables in neat rows and the trainer's table in front of the other tables. There, the trainer would compile his presentation very much based on a previous session. The date, name and location of the organisation to be trained is changed from the last one. The data projector is prepared and hot and ready to deliver a barrage of some 1000 PowerPoint slides at the retinas of the attendees. The participants begin filling the space from the back row forwards

My coach colleague and I go to our room which is adjacent to the trainer's room. We place the chairs in a harmonious circle for dialogue. The first impression is very important in the session. This is why I invest in the beginning and the atmosphere associated with it. The session space needs good feng shui, i.e. learning, is in harmony with the learning environment. It is complemented by a beautiful view of the forest landscape and the summer light of the sun. The tables are next to the walls of the room. For them, we have compiled books that fit the theme of team coaching. The theme of the day is team learning and leadership. We have selected a few key theories on the theme for the walls, visualised on flip chart sheets

We thought of a good check-in question. How can we create a good atmosphere in the learning team? We are going to play Bruce Springsteen's playlist. The trainees enter our prepared room. They start chatting with their own friend or friends while glancing at those who also come in. Their appearance speaks of slight excitement and confusion. I see them thinking inside their heads: Where am I?

I will start with an introduction to Carol S. Dweck's (2006) Mindset audiobook on learning, which I just listened to. I will tell you that success is about self-development and the pursuit of new learning: do you have a growth or fixed mindset? My coach partner ponders the goal of learning and asks: How are you doing and what book have you read about leadership or learning? Since we are only meeting for the first time, the participants do not know each other properly, even though some come from the same workplace and others work together. Unfortunately, and strangely, genuine dialogue rarely takes place in the workplace. We encourage participants to engage in dialogue. They tell key things about their own lives, thoughts and workplace. In team coaching and team learning, it is essential to highlight the themes to be discussed from the participants.

I ask who wants to be coaches of smaller project teams, i.e. junior team coaches (we use Swedish word "lilla tränäre), Four volunteers stand out from the learning team. While the others are taking a short break, we discuss with my coach colleague and the junior team coaches about what is the theme of the first training session and how we divide the participants into smaller, i.e. project teams. This is how the junior team coaches begin to take responsibility for the learning process. We emphasise that the most important thing is to build trust, which starts with genuine dialogue. We end up with the fact that in the first exercise, the training session, the project teams get to know each other and think about good management experiences and make a free-form summary before lunch. When we unpack the results of the workout in a common dialogue session, the participants exude enormous competence, mild enthusiasm and latent frustration – What can I change? The dialogue begins to come alive. The strengths and painful points of the work community are highlighted.

The participants have prepared in advance by reading books related to learning. We will consider a few theories. One of them is the importance of a learning team for learning and how it differs from a project team. My coach partner and I sit down at the same table with the junior team coaches for lunch. We reflect on how the morning went and what would be the next step. I would like to point out the beautiful weather, the possibility of a fitness trail trip and the role of a team coach – more listening, reflection and summarising in place of direct answers and advice.

My colleague asks the junior team coaches what has been written about the change in work community's strategy. Some people remember seeing a documentary. We decide that the project teams will look for one concrete thing that can improve leadership. At the same time, the work community's strategy is also examined. The junior team coaches are eager to continue their work.

I then meet the trainer from the next room for lunch, the trainer who I met first when opening my door, and I ask, how is the session going? The "coaching", i.e. the training, has reportedly gone well and they have gone through the theories of leadership. In the afternoon, the plan is to present the goals set by the management and engage the trainees. The trainer then returns to the room without actually enquiring from me anything. I, on the other hand, leave with my own coach colleague for a walk outside. There is a beautiful summer breeze. The sun is high in the sky and shining. A project team comes towards us. They have noticed our descriptions of the beautiful summer breeze. They seem to be in cheerful and joyful mood. It seems that trust in the team has been clearly achieved, and the junior trainer of the project team has been able to take on this role well.

In team coaching, it is essential to hand over your own coaching power to the project and the junior trainers. Team coaching is experiential learning. In it, the learner takes responsibility for their own learning. By doing and experiencing yourself, insights and real memory traces are created, i.e. learning takes place. In the same way, the trainees learn to function in the work community if the management only agrees to relinquish power and unnecessary control.

We go back into dialogue mode. Project teams start sharing their insights. The presentations are free form. One team has a visual flip chart. The second team puts us on the lookout for more ideas. The third team performs a touching play about how things were performed in the past and how to change what is done. The fourth team presents a short video that they have filmed. Judging from the presentations, the strategy of the work community has been unearthed. One tEeam had evidently immersed itself in the new school curriculum. We have a joint dialogue about the performances all together This exhilarates me.

Next, the project teams give feedback to their own junior team coaches. Receiving feedback is important for development. What did I succeed in and what could I develop further? My coach colleague and I will reveal the flip chart feeds for enthusiasm for the next session. Because the most important thing in coaching programs is not what happens during the coaching days themselves, but what happens between them. We share book tips as preparation instructions for the next session and encourage experimentation with team learning and team coaching.

Finally, it is time to check out. I ask the question: What changes will you make in your own activities based on this training? We go round he participants so that everyone has a chance to speak. Finally, I encourage action and recommend James Clear's book Atomic Habits. I collect my books, flip charts and walk to my car with my coach We reflect on the day, and I go through what went well in our coaching, what went badly, what we learned and what we will put into practice next time. Indeed, team coaching is always experiential learning, both for the participants and team coaches alike.

Dialogue creates self-management

The chairs form a symmetrical circle. I am nervous as a team coach. A ring has about 25 learners and two team coaches. Some of the learners are silent. There are a few happy conversations going on and one more serious one. I am able to recognise three introverts who are completely silent and stare in front of them almost in panic. From the buzz of the talking, you can sense the overall atmosphere. It is an atmosphere of anticipation.

Dialogue begins in emptiness. There are others as well as myself. I stop the talking by simply raising my hand. I will now begin talking. I will reiterate the rules of dialogue: direct speech, respect, listening and waiting.

Usually, I start by asking something simple and very open. Through my own openness I try to create a relaxed atmosphere. I succeed and the atmosphere opens up slightly. Conversation begins but slowly. I closely observe the development of dialogue. My challenge is that when I get excited about a theme, I take over the entire airtime. One of the most challenging laws of a team coach is the law of intervention: "When a team coach feels that they should intervene in a dialogue or a matter, then they should refrain from doing so". Conversely, "When you feel that you should not interfere, then you have to intervene." I seek a balance between creating a good atmosphere and remaining quiet.

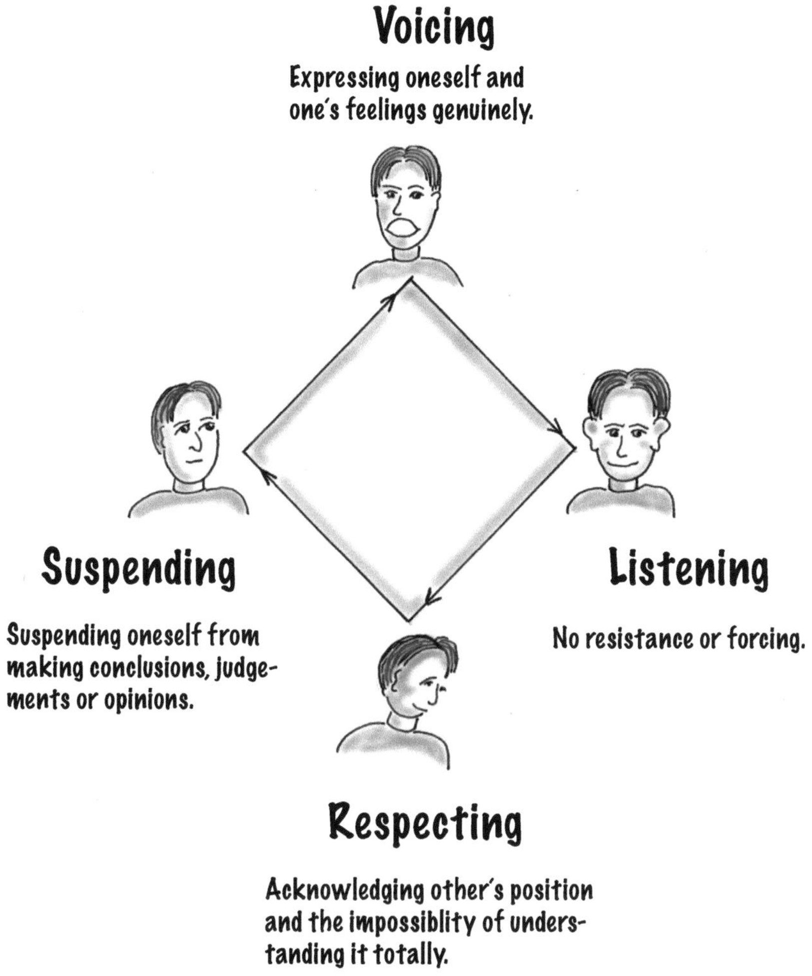

Voicing

Expressing oneself and one's feelings genuinely.

Suspending

Suspending oneself from making conclusions, judgements or opinions.

Listening

No resistance or forcing.

Respecting

Acknowledging other's position and the impossiblity of understanding it totally.

Figure 8. Rules of dialogue (Isaacs 2001).

I simply try to stick to asking. When the first introvert starts talking, the first level of trust has been established. Then I become eager, and I direct the dialogue. I say to myself in my mind: Be quiet and let others speak. After my speech, there is silence.

I decide to remain silent. I await the flow of dialogue. Now I manage to keep my mouth firmly closed. Someone asks, what are we going to put into practice about this? I respond with, who takes responsibility for learning? The team then decides to split into small groups and assign each small team an area of responsibility.

Team coaching is based on social constructionism, i.e. the communal construction of knowledge and concepts. The idea is that the information is not automatically transferred to the learner, but the learner rebuilds the knowledge based on their own needs. Learning is functional. The learner gets enthused with experimentation, questions, solutions and understanding. Situational interaction, i.e. dialogue, supports learning. The team is a tool for the learning of the individual (learner). The team and the individual strengthen each other's growth. Reflection, i.e. weighing up doing, experiencing, insights, feedback and new theory, is central.

Epistemology – The theory of knowledge

Figure 8 shows the soul of team learning by Japanese professors Ikujirō Nonaka and Hirotaka Takeuchi. It all starts with dialogue. Learners have silent information. In the first stage, information is shared in dialogue through socialisation, i.e. through talking. In the second stage, the information becomes more concise where public information, crystallises and summaries are generated. In the third stage, the information is formed into a plan that is intended to be implemented. In the fourth stage, the knowledge is tested and applied, that is to say internalised.

When dialogue flows, I try to be present. Listening in the present is always difficult. I think about the rules of dialogue and epistemology. I try to take care of the rules of dialogue so that the strength of the team is revealed. A team is at its ultimate strongest when all team members participate in one way or another.

Those who are quieter have the right to be quiet. You can sometimes read from body language when an introvert has something on their mind but are unable to say what they are thinking. It is now that the team coach is provided with the opportunity to sensitively ask the introvert for their wise idea so it can be included in the dialogue.

We can jump into practice right away. Someone or some people get up and get to work with the whole team. The circle of knowledge theory has been reversed. Even crystallisation ideas are important in dialogue. By thinking about them collectively, small teams come up with ideas for experiments and promises of practical action. Through dialogue, team learning creates joint guidance.

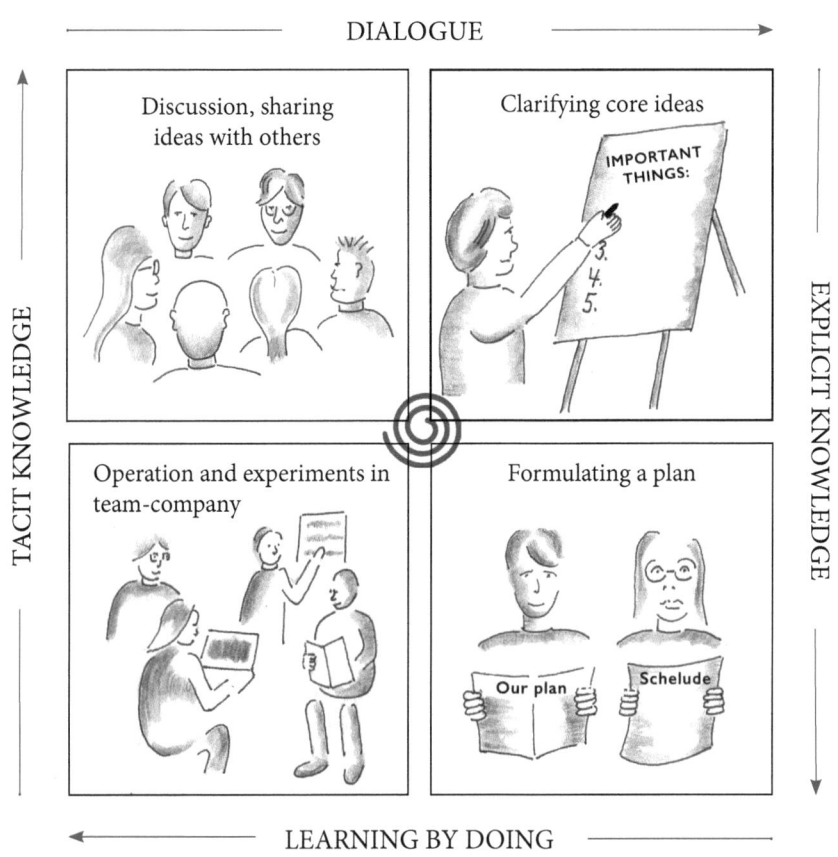

Figure 9. Epistemology (Nonaka & Takeuchi 1995)

An introvert is often able to sharply crystallise the core ideas of a dialogue lasting several hours in just a few sentences. Sometimes someone more talkative or a few extroverts dominate the airtime of dialogue. If the team is in the early stages of development and does not dare or know how to establish a balance with the airtime of extroverts' speaking time, I have handed out a ten-minute red silence card. A good question for the quieter ones also steers the dialogue in the right direction.

Epistemology is running in the back of my mind. Dialogue must turn into learning by doing. Knowledge learning is not only dialogue but also learning by doing. The team must be able to bring up the ideas for experimentation that could lead to learning by doing. Chatter is the fuel of dialogue. I observe the emerging crystallizations or experiments in In an advanced team, a plan can be created.

53

Organising team activities

Building teams requires wisdom from management to combine the organisation of operations and learning. In his book Teams of Teams, General McChrystal (2015) describes the leadership of the American war in Iraq against al-Qaeda in the early 2000s. At least in my own mind, the military is basically a hierarchical organisation, though in reality, a military organisation that always learns has won the war. War is a balancing act between complexity and adaptability. The complexity of a military organisation arises from interdependence and speed. Thousands, tens of thousands, even hundreds of thousands of soldiers are waiting for co-ordinated orders on how to act quickly and effectively. The enemy's movements are unpredictable, and they should be countered in a systematic way. The adaptability of military forces is empowering operational capability and shared awareness. This is formed by trust and a shared meaning.

According to General McChrystal (2015), Americans went to war against Al-Qaeda using the traditional hierarchical command model (command model, Figure 10). The terrorist organisation proved to be more effective against this leadership model. Next, a team management model was tested, in which the teams were independent, and management guided each team (command of teams). This model also failed to produce results. As a last resort, the Teams of Teams Model was tested, in which teams had the power over their own actions and the management of the whole. Through this model, the Americans defeated Al-Qaeda in Iraq.

If a military organisation can operate in such a team-oriented manner and distribute power to teams, how could it be impossible for other work communities? An employee-owned co-operative company would be ideologically the best possible platform for this form of management. In fact, there are a few such companies in the world, such as the Mondragon Co-operative in the Basque Country, in Spain. A co-operative is actually an association of co-operatives, which consists of about 100 smaller co-operatives. It has more than 80,000 employees and a turnover of more than 12 billion euros. The common values of co-operation, participation, social responsibility and innovation guide the operations of Mondragon's huge co-operative. One co-operative is Mondragon University – what if all universities and schools were owned by teachers?

I have a few friends who are shareholders in the Mondragon Corporation that is a world leader in the co-operative movement. As I understand it, new employees are put on a trial period of five years. After this trial period, the employee I entitled to buy a share in the co-operative for around 15 000 euros. The entire co-operative also bears responsibility for any unpleasant decisions. A few years ago, one of the co-operatives in the Mondragon consortium went bankrupt, with the result that each member of the co-operative was paid only 80 percent of their salary for a few years. The consortium has grown to become the largest company in the Basque Country and the tenth largest in Spain, which is a strong sign of the success of the operating model. A co-operative is an excellent tool for promoting the interests of the owners. The key is who the owners are, namely: producers, customers or employees. According to my own observations, an employee-owned co-operative is the best way to maintain the owners' will under control. The management of a customer - or producer - oriented co-operative can be given expert power.

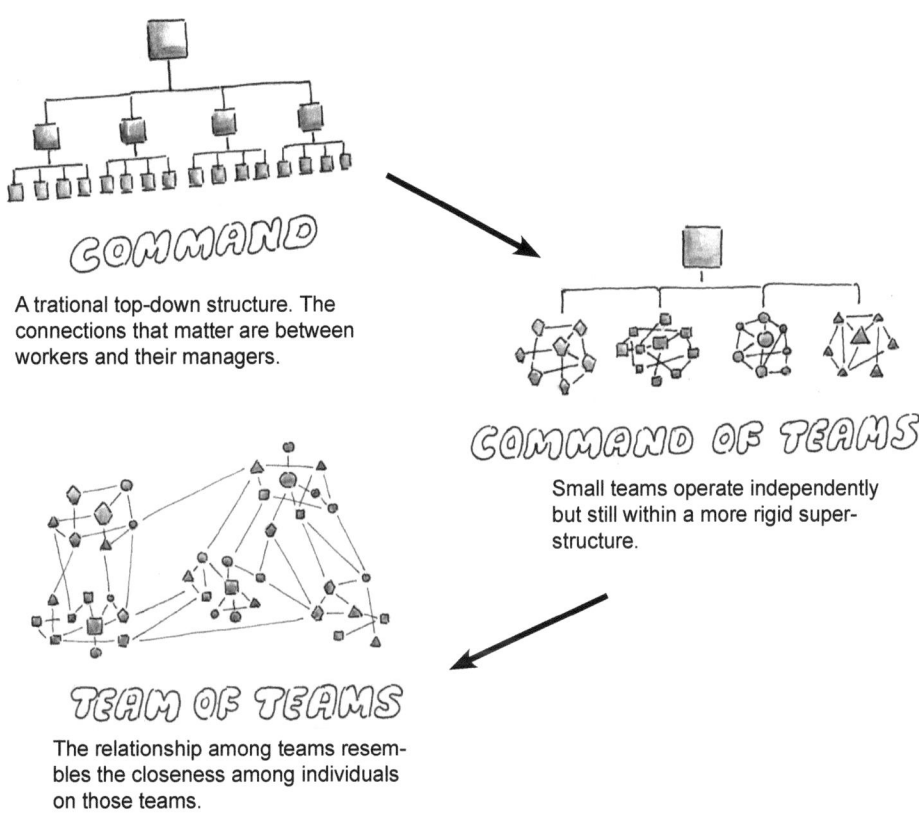

Figure 10. The command model, the command model for teams, and the Teams of Teams model (McChrystal, 2015).

4. Team coach and coaching leader

New leadership models

Gary Hamel's book, The Future of Leadership (2007), made me think about the pressures for change in leadership. Hamel believes that leadership needs to be reinvented. I am in agreement with this. The era of the old Henry Ford quarterly management system is over. We are in need of a new, modern "Taylorism" model. I argue that the new paradigm of leadership is team learning - working together, learning and leading. We need more leadership, but we need fewer leaders. Coaching leadership and people-oriented coaching have already been on the rise ever since the 1990s. Now, in the 2020s, it is time for a breakthrough.

Leadership can be divided into three factors of leadership: managing things, managing people, and coaching people. Traditionally, managing things is the most central thing – which is highly important, such as getting the customer exactly what they ordered and being able to pay the employees' salaries. In people leadership, it is essential to inspire a common vision. The learning of people is central to coaching people. You need a team to lead things, lead people, and coach people.

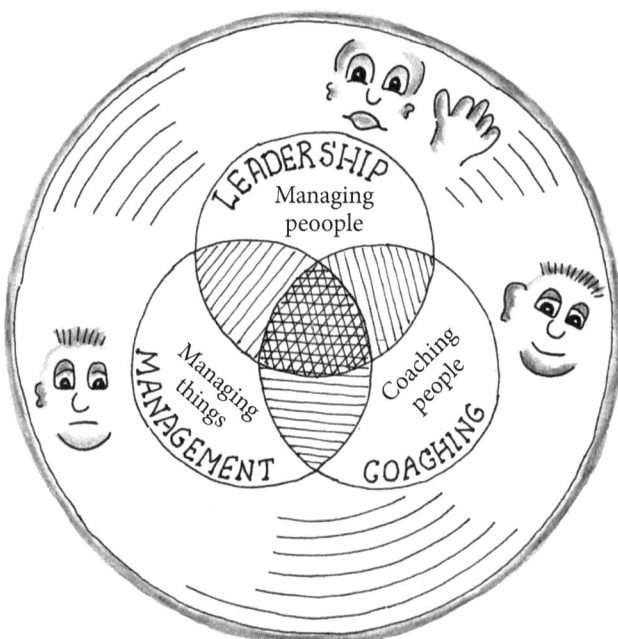

Figure 11. Managing the matters of the team, leading people and coaching teams.

The management of today's issues, i.e. the formation of strategy, is based on Porter's (1980) works on strategic choices. Porter emphasised the choice: differentiate or cut costs. The company in question therefore had to choose between these two areas. Kim and Mauborgne developed the logic of the choice further. They urged to choose the key competitive factors in the industry and stand out through them with the strategy profile of the company. Which strategic elements of the company should be created, emphasised, reduced or eliminated are described.

The pioneer in people management is Jim Collins, who in his books Build to Last (1994), Good to Great (2001) and Great by Choice (2011), creates a different type of framework for people management. There are many good authors on this subject, namely: Gary Hamel, Bob Maurer, Ian Cunningham, Peter Senge, Daniel Kahne man and John Kotter, to name just a few.

Good books on coaching are sports coaching books. Axel Ferguson, Erkka Westelund, Petteri Nykky, Henrik Dettman and Aki Hintsa, among others, have opened up to us on their coaching philosophy. Many commercial oriented books on the subject are based on coaching the individual. Among them, and very much worth mentioning are Michel Bungay's book The Coaching Habit (2016), Jari Salminen's Skilful Team Coach (2013), Marja-Riitta Ristikangas and Vesa Ristikangas's Coaching Leadership (2010), a well as Dan Soback's Coaching Leadership (2021) identically named.

In the new management model, management of issues and people, as well as coaching are combined into team coaching. The foundation of leadership is created by people and the management power given to them. The work community is given the freedom to fulfil itself. People do the things required of the work community according to a shared vision. Measuring operations plays a key role. The results of the shared vision are measured visibly and openly. The indicators must be clear enough, simple, starting from the team member and guiding to the result. Leadership is based on pair leadership, where the team coach's main responsibility is to develop the team and lead the team leader's issues.

The difference between a team coach and a coaching leader

If the coach is only responsible for the learning of the team, then they are a team coach. If the coach bears responsibility for the learning and results of the team, then they are a coaching leader.

The key role of the team coach is to build the team's learning culture and process. The team coach must be strict in following the principles of the learning culture, but at the same time be "soft" and empathetic towards the learners. Personally, I do not believe in quick coaching or training that lasts a day or two. Learning is so slow that there must be several sessions to create a longer learning process. Between these session events, there must be practical actions, reflection by small teams and acquiring theoretical knowledge though reading, listening or observing. This learning model is called process learning. The titles of coach and trainer are often mixed with talent. Many distinguished trainers call themselves coaches. When the trainer bears the responsibility for learning, the learning starts from the trainer's theories and he or she is vocal most of the time, it is wrong to call the learning event coaching or the trainer a coach.

The image below depicts the real role of a team coach. A team coach works 80 percent of the time in the field of coaching: he or she listens, reflects, reviews what has been said and asks questions, and a maximum of only 20 percent in teaching, that is to say he or she provides options, feedback, tips, instructions or advice.

In the majority of work communities, a coaching leader takes care of the learning of the team and is responsible for achieving results. It is difficult to combine them. Lear-

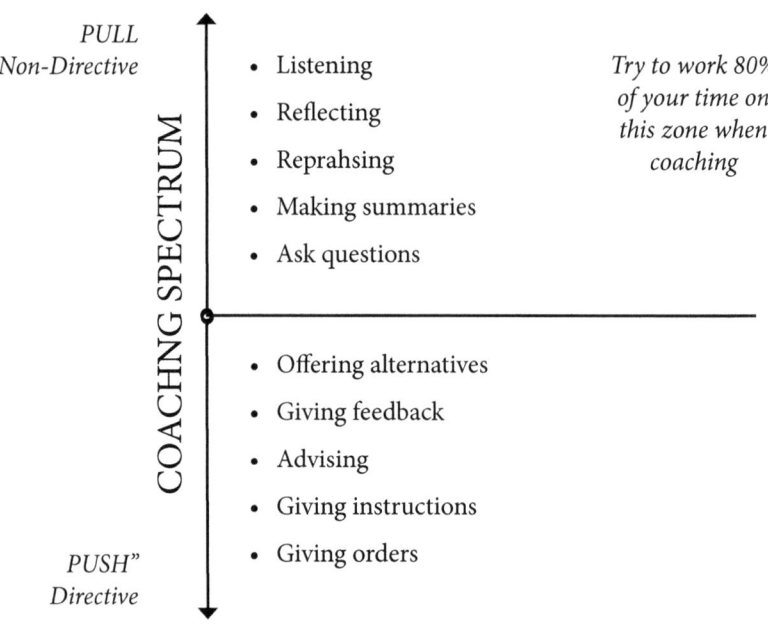

Figure 12. The team coach functions through a coaching approach.

ning is often at such a slow pace that the leader can mistakenly take the lead. I remember well the story of a team leader who had tried to guide one of her groups towards a new kind of teamworking by suggesting different alternatives and even forcing experiments. The group's opposition was fierce. Eventually, the team leader became highly frustrated and gave up. The team leader declared "Then do what is best for you." The group was astounded for a while, and nothing was heard about it for a month. Interestingly, the group took responsibility for the development of a new operating model itself, without pressure from the team leader. The group then grew into a team. So, the team made the change all by themselves and the manager was quite bewildered at how this came about.

Acceptance of varying speeds

The key to coaching leadership is to allow different speeds. The whole group is going in the same direction, but each in their own way and at their own speed. Regardless of the varying speeds, a timetable must be agreed according to which everyone must proceed. Coaching leadership starts with people, and the goal is to support their learning. A key tool in this is a learning agreement, which includes reflection on one's own past and agreeing on one's own goals. On the basis of the learning agreement, the work community provides the individual with the necessary resources to achieve the goals, which also support the development of the work community. These matters are agreed upon in development discussions.

In one work community, the management defined the elements and indicators of change. There was a total of 8-10 of them. It was agreed that after one year, 2-3 of them should be in use, after two years, 4-6, and after three years, all elements should be in use.

In traditional leadership, it is assumed that all people follow the leader's instructions immediately. Change is allowed little time meaning the time given is limited. In reality, some people follow the leader, some go their own way, and many stay completely where they are when they cannot find time for change. The change the leader is aiming for goes in a different direction than he or she would have wanted. In coaching leadership, change is given the time needed. There is a dialogue between people about this issue, and different speeds are allowed. The change is slower, but the change is permanent. Sometimes direction can change, because the wisdom of change lies in people and the intellect of the crowd or group.

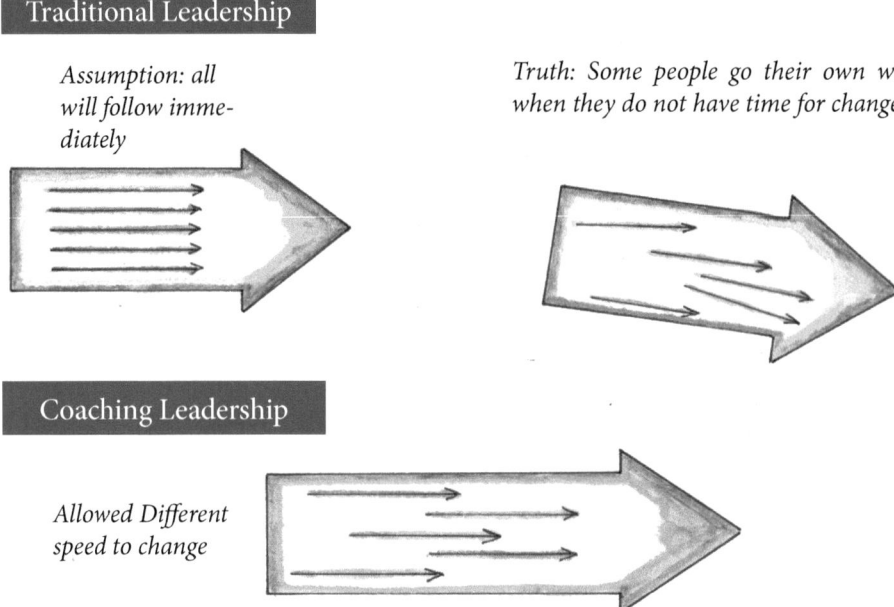

Traditional Leadership

Assumption: all will follow immediately

Truth: Some people go their own way when they do not have time for change

Coaching Leadership

Allowed Different speed to change

The large arrow depicts the state of mind of the organisation

Figure 13. Variation of creative and systematic thinking.

5. Team coaching laws

Through years of experience, Johannes Partanen developed the principles of Team coaching, which are called the Team coach Principles. The eight laws in the Principles are the deepest core of team coaching. Mastering the laws in practice is a lifelong task. These laws are also called the laws of Johannes, but I refer to them in this book Team coach Laws. These laws are also easily applied with competence in leadership or management.

5.1. The Law of Non-interference

The first team coach Law is the Law of Non-interference, which is at the very core of team coaching. When do you let a team or a team member learn through mistakes, or do mistakes occur at all?

When can you try to guide them to the right path based on experience? There are many different routes to the same destination. The power of the word of a team coach, teacher, leader, or expert can be enormous. One question, comment, statement or just a facial expression can have a huge impact. Sometimes, however, it feels like no question, comment or emotional outburst causes any reaction. When learners have their own projects, then the team coach cannot get involved in projects too deeply. For an experienced leader, this is a challenge – one's own expertise can feel superior. An experienced leader should focus on thinking about and listening to good questions. The team coach builds a learning process for the team and its members, which is different for each team and person. It is good to keep the learning process in mind before intervening. You have to think about what stage the team is at the teaming process and where the team is going. It is also important to have your own coach persona, i.e. character – which is the trait of your own personality that helps the team develop further.

In team coaching, we always have two coaches. For example, when one becomes excited about the trees, the other can just observe. The mutual reflection of the team coaches helps to notice the points of intervention and non-intervention in the dialogue. It is difficult to notice them in an instant. In some cases, this reflection brings up issues that still need to be addressed. Especially in remote coaching, the speaker does not have time to notice the reactions of everyone. In one coaching session, my partner coach asked me afterwards, did you notice how that one participant felt like an outsider? I hadn't noticed it myself. At check-out, however, the participant revealed a level of scepticism and asked, "Is this the right way for me to learn?" Based on the reflection with two coaches, we evaluated that the person had been strongly guided to participate in the Team Mastery coaching program.

The composition of the project team that this hesitant participant was part of did not support his professional identity. We subsequently changed the person to another team with success and the participant was able to flourish in a different way. In this case, an intervention helped.

In the flow of coaching, the Law of Non-interference works:

> *Do not intervene when you feel you should. Intervene when you feel that you should not intervene. When thinking about this, you remain very present at the core of dialogue, team coaching or leadership.*

In my own doctoral dissertation on the paper and pulp machine industry, I noticed that top management interfered in matters that they really should not have interfered with. Hierarchical management heaps power on the top management. It easily uses this power, even if it does not understand what is at stake. The competitive atmosphere of the top management team also leads to the management not asking for the opinion of others but acting completely alone. For example, The CEO of a company went alone to mediate a difficult complaint with a customer. This mediation trip cost hundreds of millions of Euros.

5.2. Slow Learning

The slowness of learning is staggering. Changing mindsets and learning new things requires patience from both the learner and the team coach. In a team, learning is faster and more efficient.

The learner receives 360-degree feedback on their own work continuously from their peers, customers, team coach and the leader of their own team. A team is a tool for individual learning. The tighter the team works, the better the individual learns. The learning team must be long-term. Personally, I only believe in process learning, i.e. a process that lasts at least four months, during which you can get a new direction for your own learning. Preferably a little longer, such as the Team Mastery process, which lasts a year and a half.

Saku Tuominen, who is a successful Finnish TV producer, entrepreneur and non-fiction writer wrote Creative Reasoning (2014) in which what is needed in change is looked at:

1. The ability to see (one's own development needs),

2. the desire to do something with them,

3. a little better,

4. much better.

"Much better", i.e. making disruptive changes, is really challenging. Much better is created from many "a little better" activity. The Japanese Kaizen principle depicts this, i.e. continuous small and determined improvements, leads to change. A good change is one that you can make right away, benefits the customer, and costs nothing. There are many Kaizen books, I personally like Mauer's (2012) book The Sprit of Kaizen. The motivation for learning and the goals for learning are very important. Making a learning agreement and explaining its goals to other team members guides the team to help the individual move forward.

Slow learning produces better learning outcomes. Pasi Sahlberg (2015) analyses the strengths of the Finnish school system as follows:

1. Strong competence of teachers,

2. local curricula,

3. competition-free learning.

Point three refers to building a learning path that starts with the learners and is unique to each individual, i.e. slow learning. An even deeper book that emphasises the slowness of learning is Kotvimisen Vallankumous or the Deliberation Revolution (Kangasvuo, Pulkkinen & Rauanjoki 2018). This book, not available in English, unfortunately, advises you to take a break that is essential to work, because without a break, the work will not be completed or developed. The book argues that co-operation is one of the significant pillars and advantages of Finnish comprehensive schools compared to comprehensive schools in other countries.

For me, the slowness of learning is self-evident. I have mild dyslexia, so learning languages is really slow. My mother, who was a Finnish language teacher, suggested that I go to a vocational college, but I didn't want to. I wanted to force myself into high school. At least I was very good at maths. In high school, I had great difficulties with languages and once dropped out of my class due to poor language performance. During one class session, one of my classmates brought me some notes which had been useful in studying for the Swedish exam the night before and where my class got grade eight. I studied the notes for one week and got grade five. Part of the poor language performance may have been due to the motivation, or lack of it. I thought that mathematics and the management philosophy of the South Savo would suffice for me. I recall when I succeeded in getting into the Otaniemi University of Technology in Finland I went to eat in the canteen ran by the Swedish Student Society. I was quite surprised to notice that everyone only spoke Swedish. I actually realised that I had to learn Swedish and English so well that I could also manage in these foreign languages.

I took language courses, but my success was poor. Traditional language teaching did not suit me. I found I learned by doing. I first applied for a summer job in Sweden at

Volvo. I vividly remember sitting in the HR leader's room where I understood perhaps 30 per cent of what was being said. The fact that my language skills were quite poor ton say the least I thought to myself what are you doing here? Nonetheless, I managed so much that I was actually offered a job after that summer.

The following summer, I was off to Canada to work at a foundry. A similar start, but the foundry had asked for more technology students from the Otaniemi Universty to train at the end of the summer. In the next phase, I applied to the English-language Linkage program for a year. Then I made my master's thesis in English. This allowed me to work in Japan for three years. As a result of this long-term work, I am able to handle business matters fluently in English and reasonably in Swedish. Evidence of this is the company acquisition process that I began in my advanced pidgin English in the USA. I find myself still getting my words mixed up from time to time, and my spelling contains a significant number of mistakes, but I can take care of business quite proficiently.

5.3. The Law of The Thin Red Thread

Team learning is based on socio-constructivism. Learning starts with the learners and the learning process is built around their needs. This is why the check-in round is very important, as is genuinely listening to expectations. Through this, learners express their goals.

The Team coach must have some idea of the learning process as a whole. The saying "trust the process but never trust the process" is sage advice. Similarly, "trust the process – tolerate lack of clarity and chaos".

When learners finally build the learning process for themselves, the team coach must create security and trust. Certain principles, such as the rules of dialogue, dialogue sessions, learning by doing, reading books and/or listening, are adhered to in the creation of a learning agreement. However, when learners are different and their needs are different, I can never know what is right and what is wrong. The learning process can sometimes go wrong, and this is when we all learn. It is essential to share a common vision, i.e. a goal for the entire process, a goal to which everyone commits.

I vividly remember when I participated in the sixth team master training. I had the honour of working as a coach of a small team in a three-day session, i.e. "junior trainer". Johannes Partanen, the main developer of the method, acted as a coach for the process. He was very enthusiastic about the development of the Team Mastery training and the fact that representatives and leaders from the business world were involved. At the end of the training, on Saturday, the birthday of the Team Academy was announced. Philosopher Esa Saarinen was about to be the keynote speaker and Johannes wanted to present the new innovation to Esa. Then Johannes got the idea that we, the team master students, would present the "birth", i.e. our final crystallisation, in a fun and vivid form at the Team Academy's anniversary seminar.

Johannes wished that we would make a joint presentation for the seminar. We started a dialogue about it at eight o'clock in the evening of the second day. The dialogue lasted for three hours, but no common vision was reached. All three teams withdrew to their own locations at 11 p.m. Together with another team, we decided to make our own presentations. We made them ready at one o'clock in the morning. The third team did not get anything achieved. More than 100 people participated in the seminar. Our perceptions of the coaching leadership theme turned out to be very different. My own small team performed really well, the second one did reasonably well, and the third one was quite at sea, that is to say lost.

Around this time, Gary Hamel's book The Future of Leadership had been published, in which Hamel criticised modern leadership. Hamel thinks Henry Ford could lead any listed company with a two-week induction. The team I was part of made a striking performance. One member of the team played the role of a crucified leader who died and was reborn. In my opinion, our presentation was a great success. Personally, I learned three things during this coaching session: let the learners act independently in an unclear situation and build their own thread; a vision cannot be shared by force, and without a common, shared vision, you will get nowhere; I see that I am a pretty good coaching leader. I also realised that I wanted to be an entrepreneur and a business leader.

5.4. The Learning Environment Act

Team Academy was started in classroom 147 at the Jyväskylä University of Applied Sciences campus in 1993. Quite soon after its establishment, Team Academy moved to the old Headquarter building of the former Schauman Plywood Factor that had been refurbished, and then on to larger refurbished premises of the former Schauman Plywood Factory. The learning environment was completely different from that of a regular business school. Dialogue spaces, home bases for teams, a stage, quiet work facilities and bookable meeting rooms were constructed in the old plywood factory.

Companies have finally begun to understand the importance of the work environment for the creation of a sense of community. We need new kinds of workspaces where employees, entrepreneurs and artists from different fields meet. Old-fashioned cubicles do not support creativity and interaction. In a good communal workspace, people meet randomly and on their own initiative. The same philosophy has been used to design Proakatemia, the first "offspring" of Team Academy in Tampere, Finland.

Proakatemia was located in the old factory premises in the Finlayson area of Tampere in Finland. The learning environment was on the top floor, with a great view of the Tammerkoski rapids that ae part of the city of Tampere's environment. When the customer is close to the learning environment, it is easy to visit them. The learning environment must enable formal and informal encounters between learners. It should also take into account different types of individuals. An introvert wants peace and an extrovert wants action. The law of the learning environment also affects why we organise our team coaching sessions at a farm tourism site. Over the years, we have chosen suitable places with a good space for dialogue, meeting rooms for small teams, an excellent sauna, hot tub and swimming area, sports facilities, smooth service, good food and comfortable accommodation rooms. In the learning environment, it is also important to take into account variation: if the team needs new inspiration, then working in different places bring about a much-needed change to the rhythm. For me, it is important to have a harmonious balance which is where fengsui is important. Fengsui means that the learning environment is in harmony with the learners. An example of this is the positioning of the chairs of a dialogue circle. I want the chairs to form a regular circle, because it symbolises the equality of dialogue.

In 2015, I participated in the New Education Forum organised by the Finnish Innovation Fund called Sitra. Sitra had invited a little over thirty learning specialists to participate in a year-long coaching process to share new practices and develop a vision for learning for Finland. The vision became: A country where everyone loves learning. This is when we got the idea in 2016 to rethink the learning environments of vocational colleges. Helsinki Business College, Helsinki Vocational College and Kamppi Shopping Centre joined us in the project. We took 35 students to the Team Academy Factory, which we named the Pop-Up College, that was established in a shopping centre for two months. The learning results were excellent including many students who were at risk of dropping out of studies actually managing to succeed and complete their degrees. We received the Special Chair's Global Best Award for this in the field of education, i.e. the International Education Business Partnership (IPN). We received this in Oslo together with the Helsinki Vocational College and the Helsinki Business College. The learning environment was completely new and was excellent for team learning. In summary:

- Seven professional sectors: baker-confectioner, cook, print communications, interior design, milliner, tourism and business administration.
- Certificates of employment for 30 students (16+14), pass rate 77 per cent.
- 1160 competence points (430+730), i.e. 39 credits/student/2 months.
- Approximately 500 guests.
- More than 130 customer visits by students to the business community.
- Kamppi Shopping Centre in Helsinki was very satisfied with the pilot.

5.5. The Law of The Team Coach 's Own Role

In my opinion, this law boils down to this thought: I am more than an acquaintance, but less than a close friend, i.e. I am a buddy or a friend.

This same principle applies perfectly to leadership. Friendship requires that the team coach knows the person they are coaching well enough. Continuous development or successful discussions, and the learner's learning agreement discussed in connection with them, help the team coach to get to know the learner. Knowing the learner to the level of friendship causes an unequal position in the team. Fostering a learning culture requires movement skilfully within and outside the team. Sometimes you have to dive into the flow of the team and sometimes look at the activities from a little afar. You should stay out of projects and customer relationships. If the team coach mistakenly takes responsibility for the projects, the learner moves aside. This is a challenge in co-operatives for people under the age of 18, as the law states that companies, i.e. co-operatives, must have adults. Fortunately, there is a Junior Achievement concept in Finland, which enables entrepreneurship for minors. Sometimes there may be learners in the team who simply do not fit in with the team coach in terms of personal chemistry. Then you can keep in mind the sentence: I do not have to be a close friend, just being a buddy or a friend will suffice.

When a team coach is in charge of the learning process, their leadership position can rise too high. A good leader is able to engage in dialogue with everyone in a respectful manner. I remember meeting Martin Saarikangas, the visionary shipyard leader and founder of Masa Yards in Finland during a party at the Japanese Embassy in Tokyo. Martin is a tall man, over 190 centimetres tall, seemingly a giant compared to the Japanese delegates at the embassy. Masa Yards had received a significant ship order from Japan. Martin patiently toured each guest and genuinely asked how everyone was doing, including myself, a young businessman who had just graduated. I vividly remember when a young Japanese businessman who was next to me responded to Martin's simple question by muttering something general in unambiguously bad English. Martin, realising the unease, asked a follow-up question and then took care to attentively listened which made the young Japanese person relax. This is how a real leader and team coach works. She or he makes learners relax and be the best editions of themselves.

5.6. Customer Relations Act

The customer must always be at the heart of team activities. "The more meetings, the more offers". This sentence describes the mathematics of customer relationships. The more you interact with the customer, the more meaningful the end and the more developed the operations of the team will be.

The team coach must think about the value of the customer chain a few steps ahead of the customers in the team. First, see your own team and the team members, i.e. the learners, who are the customers of you, the team coach. Coaches should serve their customers to their maximum ability. Secondly, the customers, who are the learners, must be taken into full account by the coaches during their coaching work. Then there are the external clients that can be in the form of companies, parents, private individuals, from working life or work communities. The team coach must fully encourage the learners to interact with their own customers as much as possible.

In the world of educational institutions, own customer relationships of learners are related to their future goals, dreams and development. The team coach must take into full account the level of development of each learner, i.e. how deeply the learner can focus on their own customer relationships and how the customer relationships take them forward on the path of learning.

I think that in every work community, everyone should have three types of customers and projects:

1. Money projects, i.e. current customers who earn their living,

2. communal projects, i.e. internal customer relationships that develop the community further, and

3. future dream projects and customer relationships that support your own development and future activities. The task of team coach es is to guide, by using questions, the customer so he or she is genuinely at the heart of development. In this case, there is a real need for learning. The customer relationships of these three different project types must be in balance.

The most important thing is that all learners have real external clients. It is not common to get in touch with a stranger who would be disgusted to ask for money for the products or services they offer, as well as information or help to make their dream come true. The composition of the project team plays an important role in this. There should always be one person in the project team who has the courage to contact external clients. This contact with external clients must be continuous. Chet Holmes advises in his excellent sales book The Ultimate Sales Machine that the CEO of a small company such as I should spend two hours a day on business development, including cold calls to potential customers. As a team coach at the Team Academy, I paid attention to the cost structure of the projects of the learners. The share of fixed costs must be kept to a minimum for a start-up company and the main focus must be fluctuating. In this case, starting a project is easy, and as the volume grows, the operations develop healthily.

I vividly remember a rather large event project where three learners, i.e. the team entrepreneurs, who had just started learning at Team Academy, desperately wanted to carry out. It became aware to me that the fixed costs of the event were some 10,000 Euros, and there were only about two months left until the start of the event was due. I suggested a meeting after the dialogue session, during which we made a sales plan together and put it into practice immediately. I succeeded in encouraging them to look for customers and potential financiers without delay. After a week, they themselves realised and stated that they have too much of a tight schedule and there is no time to get enough customers. As a result, they were able to reduce their own loss to about 1,000 Euros and they were wise to postpone the project by a year enabling a realistic time schedule. With the aid of the realistic time schedule, the project was realised final realised and with was a huge success.

5.7. The Law of Interference

The Team coach must always intervene in the team's situation when it is a question of safety, a disturbance that hinders the activities of the team, bullying, great sadness or overwhelming happiness. Johannes's instruction reads: "You show the way because you care. You show love and care."

This builds a culture of trust in the team. I have often been in a situation where the trust in the team has grown so great that a learner has revealed their own personal great sadness. Almost the entire team may have then started crying, and as a team coach, I hug the learner appropriately and ask him or her to continue. The team understands the vulnerability of the learner. Often, the learner stays in the conversation, because being together gives them strength. In this case, they must be given peace and a feeling of security to be themselves. It is very common for many learners to just stay silent in situations like this.

When we focus on dialogue, electronic devices such as phones, computers and tablets must be turned off. An experienced learner will announce before the dialogue session that they are waiting for an important call or message that needs to be answered when the call comes. In this case, the team understands the interruption. If the learner does not understand the requirement to be involved deeply in the dialogue and breaks the no electronic device rule, then the team coach must intervene. In particular, the era of remote learning has highlighted the challenges of working life at many times, or as it is called, the results of multitasking, or as some say multifailing. I have often been confused by the multiband participation of participants who work remotely. Learners have developed a wonderful idea that a person can do many things at the same time. This is a fallacy and the truth is "No, you cannot effectively do many things at the same time". A person can only do one thing effectively at a time. The learner is unable to effectively participate in a dialogue, read emails and glance at a related article at the same time.

5.8. The Law of Rhythm

A team coach can think of their own role as akin to that of an orchestra conductor. Your own team is like an orchestra – what kind of orchestra and musical style suits your own team?

The state of mind of the learner and the stage of the process affect the selection of the appropriate rhythm. The principle is that fast is after slow, and slow is after fast.

The rhythm of the team affects the energy and focus of the team. Sometimes a good dialogue sinks into deep waters when philosophical questions take over. In this case, the dialogue is deep and slow. In team learning, epistemology is very important. Tacit knowledge becomes open knowledge through dialogue. The open knowledge is used to form the ideas for the experiment, which will then be trialled in practice. Mere dialogue remains light without the idea of experimentation and practical learning. Encouraging learners to try a change in rhythm can take team dialogue to a new and higher level. Sometimes the dialogue and action of the team lacks coherence without proper focus and thought. Calming dialogue clarifies thoughts.

In long Team Mastery trainings, we focus on one theme for two days. When I have this much time, I can usually calm my own mind and find a suitable rhythm for the team. Shorter coaching sessions, however, are more demanding. On the Team Academy scale, one-day coaching is short. On one occasion, I coached a colleague for short coaching. I vividly remember when I had somehow drifted into a rather quick tempo and I had become overly systematic, with a lively rhythm. I consulted with my fellow coach after the session about how best to proceed in future sessions, the suggestion was good in that it was recommended that I start slowly in the check-in round and carry out calm internal discussion in the project teams. With the knowledge that everyone gets to make their own mistakes and learn through them, I think to myself what the day might bring. During another session, already during check-in, I noticed that this slower and calmer style works. At the end of the day, the whole team thanked them for calming down and for the discussions within the project teams. This was a good teaching rhythm for me. Sometimes during long coaching, I start with a quick exercise, which gives the whole two-day session an energetic start.

5.9. Team Coach Thinking and Preparation

When the team coach adopts the mindset of a service providing leader, the team members, i.e. the learners, are the customers of the team coach, and therefore the team coach must serve his or her customers. Challenging your own and others' mindsets is at the core of team coaching. Broadening the mind is well illustrated by looking out to sea or ocean. When you look at the horizon, you can see the possible directions of life. If you

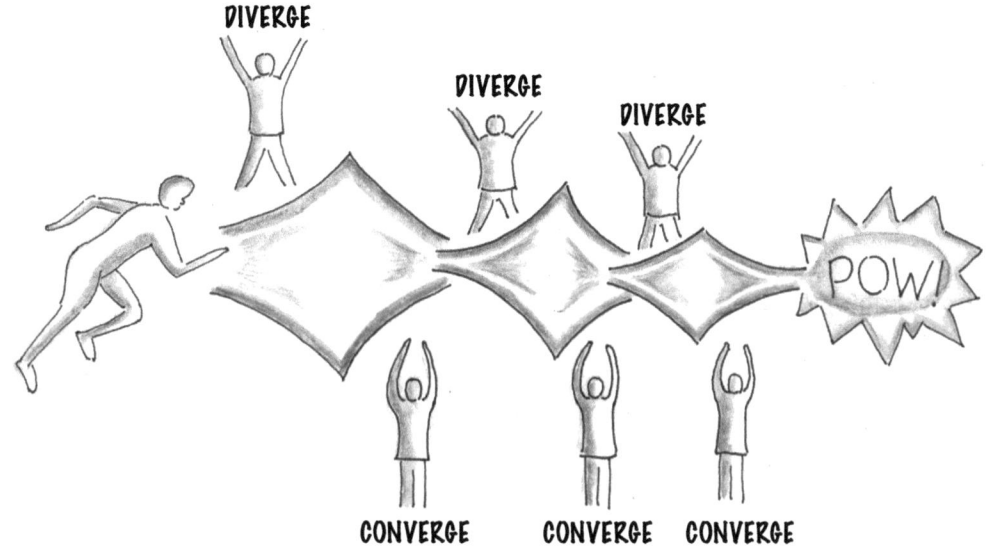

Figure 14. Variation of creative and systematic thinking.

imagine yourself as a seafarer, the possibilities that the sea or ocean hold are endless. Some kind of map, or your learning agreement, will help you find your way. Even a small change in your life will bring about a huge change on the horizon.

In team coaching, you sometimes have to broaden your thinking, i.e. diverge. Divergent thinking creates new questions, viewpoints and alternative solutions, and creativity flows. Getting to practical actions and making summaries sometimes requires convergent thinking, which is systematic, constrictive and answers individual questions that crystalise thoughts. Divergent and convergent thinking alternate. They should, however, be in balance. The challenge for work communities is that there is excessive convergence. Wider thinking would lead to better results. Nobel laureate Albert Einstein is reported to have said: "If I had an hour to solve a problem, I would spend 55 minutes thinking about the problem and five minutes thinking about solutions." In work communities, the opposite is the usual.

6. Socrates and the competencies of a team coach

The role model for a team coach can be considered as the Greek philosopher Socrates and his thinking. In the first stage, Socrates pretends to be ignorant and asks the learner to teach him about something. Socrates continues to ask questions and ask for more information until the learner realises his or her shortcomings in the matter (divergence). In the second stage, Socrates continues to ask questions until he finally brings new perspectives to the matter that crystallise the thoughts (convergence). According to Socrates, the knowledge of truth, or wisdom, is hidden in all of us. Socrates calls this method the midwifery method. The learner "generates" the thoughts themselves and learns at the same time. This becomes the term childbirth used in team learning, which combines acquired theory, new knowledge and the planning of a practical experiment and one's own modelling.

The values of Socratic method include personal mastery, surprise, encounter, and play. Peter Senge (1990) highlighted personal mastery as one of the cornerstones of a learning organisation. Each learner must strive for their own personal flourishing to the extent that it is reasonable in the opinion of each learner.

We ourselves set our own limits to development. Socrates was a startling man of his time and a reformer of thought. Too often, our thinking goes around the same loop. We would like to see new perspectives and new ways of thinking. A good team coach can startle. A genuine encounter with a learner is the starting point for dialogue. We too easily have preconceived expectations and related thoughts. The basis of team coaching is intently listening to the learner just as they are listening to the coaching they are receiving. Learning should be seen as play, joy and pleasure. Maintaining ease and lightness in the learning process brings the flow of information to learning. These four values of mastering, startling, encountering and playing, are perfect for the team coach's leading thoughts.

In business and education, lessons are learned from sports, and especially from sports coaches. The books by Erkka Westerlund, Henrik Dettmann, Petteri Nykky, and Aki Hintsa about their coaching philosophies are inspiring to read. The job description of a sports coach can be compared to the job description of a coaching manager, both are responsible for the team's results and learning. Everyone has their own coaching philosophy, but they are united by a people-oriented attitude towards each player in the team. However, putting together and coaching a team of top athletes is different from that of a work community. For example, in the annual world championship ice hockey competition, there is often only a few days before actual competitions begin when all the team is present which means actual coaching of the national team is very short. Erkka Westerlund told how he prepared a national team for the whole year, but the final selected team arrived at the Olympics just a few days before the first game. The team had to be born in a very short time. I have always imagined that it takes a long time to build a team.

At the Sochi Olympics, the ice hockey legend Teemu Selänne gave a speech to the team. The words of Teemu were so thrilling that the team actually became a team after just 15 minutes of his speech. A shared vision was born for the team. This team went on to win the Olympic bronze medal. However, behind this speech was the work of Erkka and his coaching team for almost a year. They had thoroughly studied the opposing teams. They had been intensively thinking about the composition of the team, is way of playing and principles. The coaching team had naturally had numerous discussions with the players before the selection. Looking at this from the perspective of business life, there is clear room for development in the way business life is conducted. Too many managers come to the meeting looking very relaxed, even though their familiarity with this issue or item is lacking. The composition of the team has often been formed by chance, based on levels of expertise. It can be said work communities should be more prepared for team building and development. Each team should also have its own team coach.

About the competencies of a Team coach

We have considered and developed the team coach's competence profile, which consists of ten different areas: professional experience, the object of coaching, self-development, team coaching competence, team performance coaching, individual coaching competence, planning, development and consulting competence, theoretical competence, network capital, ethics and values.

The first competence of a team coach is professional experience, and it can only be developed through the practice of doing and experimenting. The team coach must understand the context in which the team operates. Professional experience in the team's area of activity lays firmly at the foundation for competencies.

The team coach's task is to encourage the team to seize the opportunities brought about by the changes at the right time. This must be achieved in the correct way. Acting as a team coach or coaching leader requires courage to change one's own way of working and adopt team learning methods. The operating environment and colleagues do not always support new ways of working, because the old operating model has become over entrenched, and it is easier and more convenient to operate according to the old model. Your own team members or learners tend not to know how to take responsibility in the beginning for their own learning. The spaces may not even allow for dialogue. One management team planned to remove the oak tables in the corner room to make way for the dialogue circle, but their courage failed, and the oak tables remained.

Team coaching is not about trying out a collection of tricks for one session, but team coaching is long-term, and this includes the long-term building of trust. In a year, you start to see results and the team coach learns coaching. In this time, mistakes are naturally made and corrected.

Another competence is the ability to develop oneself. The most important tool in this is the learning agreement. It is a plan for one's own learning and agreeing on it with one's own team and supervisor.

A team coach must set an example for their own team. They must have the ability to see their own development needs and the desire to do something about them. The apprenticeship agreement must take into account a short time span (six months) and a longer time span (two to ten years).

The third competence is team coaching competence. The team coach must perceive the stages of the team's life cycle, coach in a manner that best suits and transform into different roles with the team.

The use of a dialogue approach is very central. The most important thing is to identify your own coaching philosophy and be able to use the key elements of team coaching: dialogue sessions, learning by doing, and reading (or information gathering). A team coach knows how to promote learning to learn in the team and to get the team enthused about learning.

The fourth area of expertise is the ability to coach the performance of the team. Leadership must be built internally in the team so that the team coach can focus on the learning process and the team can focus on doing things.

Team leadership and dialogic mentoring of potential management teams requires a masterful eye. The team coach must spar with the team to set, achieve and monitor its own performance goals. It must have short-term and long-term goals. The team must set its own goals. This requires the team coach to be able to get the team members to understand the importance of their own goals. The team must identify the strengths and knowledge capital of the members. The coach must relate the goals to the team's area of operation. This all means the team coach must have a broad understanding of the team's operating environment and its context.

The fifth competence is coaching individual competence.

The team serves as a tool for individual learning. A High-performing team consists of a variety of top individuals. A team coach is able to coach team members to learn, develop, and act in accordance with both their own and the team's goals. The systematic and open processing of the learning agreements of each team member of the team creates the basis for the development of personal mastery. Visual measurement of learning objectives supports this. The team's capabilities and personalities make up the team's intellectual capital and thus its goals. The development of learning of each team member requires joint development discussions, which are guided by the team coach and the team leader.

The sixth competence is design competence, or in historical terms, design, development and consulting competence.

The planning of coaching processes starts with the team's needs, skills and the goals of the provider. Team coaching processes have certain laws, such as the frequency of dialogue sessions, learning by doing, and gathering information for the needs of the learners by reading physical books or audiobooks. The coached team and its special requirements shape the long-term coaching process into a unique special one. The team coach must be able to build the process around these needs.

The theoretical competence of a team coach consists of team learning, team coaching, team entrepreneurship, team activities and team leadership. Theoretical knowledge and the ability to apply theories in coaching your own team are important. The team coach must be able to recommend suitable books to their own team. Constant reading of appropriate literature or listening to audiobooks should be routine for a team coach.

The team works in its own network. Working in it enables the team to develop and flourish. The more efficiently the team adds value to the network, the better it will succeed. The team coach must have an understanding of what the team needs online. The own network of colleagues supports the self-development of the team coach .

Team coaches must operate on a high ethical level. We hope that they follow the leading ideas of the Team Academy Global, which include values, vision and mission. Our mission is to create bold team coach es. The vision is to make Finland the most team-learning country in the world - I assume that we have reached the vision: there are more than 2000 trained team coaches in Finland. We need to make a new vision. The values are confidential relationships, team entrepreneurship, continuous experimentation, learning by doing and the world. The team coach must have the ability to build and coach the common goals and rules of the team. The coach guides the development of leading ideas of the team. It is crucial that the leading ideas actually come from the team and not the coach.

Be tough in a learning culture – soft on people

Shifting responsibility to learners and the team does not require the permitting of bad results. Constructing a culture of learning is based on goals, leading thoughts, principles and performance goals set by the team itself. Sometimes the goals can be very large, in which case they should be deconstructed into suitable sized pieces. As a visual person, I appreciate the visualisation of indicators, their display and continuous monitoring. Before the pandemic, I liked the indictors on the wall of our very own team's workspace or coffee room. Nowadays, the indicators on the opening page of the shared digital workspace work best. Making the indicators inspiring requires insight from the team coach and team leader, as well as the insightfulness of the team.

Regarding the goals, principles and leading ideas (vision, values, mission) defined by the team itself, the team coach must be careful and, if necessary, strict.

People must be understood and listened to from their own starting points. Individual life situations change, including occasional weak and stronger moments. The team can and should be supportive of and encourage team members in their moments of weakness. This can only be achieved when the team itself is strong. The team may also have its own weak moments, leading to much required support. A proficient team coach helps to build the right kind of team culture. In this case, we are dealing with ethical principles.

A team coach cannot take on the leadership of a team. Therefore, they must be able to successfully engage and stimulate the team with the correct questions, stories, listening, reviewing and crystallising what has been said. A situation analysis or summary is an effective means of intervention. I have often observed that a person or a team is unable to assess their own condition. The best way is to make the team evaluate themselves. The assessment tool or method depends on the needs of the team. If the team's challenge lies in issues, then the book Blue Sea Strategy (Kim and Maubourge 2005) provides an excellent framework for building team culture. If the challenge is in the team's own activities, the hedgehog concept presented in the Jim Collins book Good to Great (Collins 2001) will be of help. The hedgehog concept includes three questions:

- What inspires us/me,
- where can/can I be the best in my own area, and
- what is my/our revenue logic.

The Rauno Korpi's circle theory, which was presented earlier in building team members' knowledge, strengths and team cooperation, works superbly. I will return to this at a later stage.

In maintaining the learning culture, I am careful about the roundness of the circle of dialogue. For me, it represents the equality and non-discrimination of learners. Everyone is on the same level. I often wonder how to make a part of the circle to apply to a flip chart. I want everyone to see it in the same way. We once encountered a situation where a person in a leading position, in the company they work at, refused to join the dialogue circle they should be part of. This person decided they want to just observe the colleagues in the dialogue circle and from behind a computer. Despite several requests, the person did not want to put themself on an equal footing with others. Our team coach did not compromise and maintained the requirement to be part of the dialogue circle, but the leader flatly refused to enter any dialogue circle. As a result of the team coach insistence on the person being part of the dialogue circle, we were refused co-operation with this organisation for a couple of years. This person actually questioned dialogical leadership, fairness and team learning in their very own work community. The issue went to the Board of Directors of the work company who made the decision that the CEO is to carry out an examination of the dynamics of their work community. Further to this, the board convened and came to the conclusion that this person, who refused to join the dialogue circle, is not able to build a culture of equality and non-discrimination among the work community. On a good note, we successfully returned to partner with the company after the break of a couple of years.

As a team coach, I want to set an example of equality by always being on the same level as the learners. I will take the worst chair in the dialogue circle and ensure that the circle is kept as a perfect circle. It is my common practice to always ask coaching locations in advance to arrange the chairs in a perfect circle enabling effective dialogue.

In nursery daycare centres, chairs are often in the form of a U so that the kindergarten teacher puts themselves above the children, even though they do not have to be. On one occasion at a training location, a dialogue circle had been set up before we arrived. The Team coach 's chair was slightly better than the others and the form was not as a circle but in a U form, despite me having requested a perfect equal dialogue circle in advance. Naturally, before I started team coaching, I reorganised the chairs into a harmonious and equal dialogue circle. Equality in remote learning means that everyone has a camera on and everyone can fit on the screen - in the so-called birdhouse dialogue.

7. The beginning is the most important thing

The team is built on differences – with different tests, you get to know yourself

A good team has different personalities that complement each other. Team building begins with strengthening the team with different personalities, investing in the start, clearing minds and highlighting the long-term path of the team. This will get you started with teamwork. Any team can become a top team. Learning must be supported through increasing team competence. Through this, the development of the personal mastery of individuals is supported. Increasing competence provides concrete tools and means to implement cultural change.

It is good if you get to influence what kind of individuals make up the team. It is often thought that similarity would be good. In this case, the elected ones would be similar to each other, think and act in the same way and would be almost the same age. The future team leader tends to choose people like themselves, and people like them want similar types as teammates. This easily creates a work team that is free of tension, smiling and enjoys the company of each other, but this situation does not work miracles.

It may seem like a contradictory idea that a team should be formed with diversity. You have to choose different people with a wide range of skills, different ways of working, as well as a wide range of age demographic. In such a team, individuals must first learn to understand and tolerate differences and learn to get along with other people. When the mental patterns that hinder the activities are crushed, the differences begin to produce results and synergistic activities are created. The results of which can be quite amazing.

Just for the sake of invigorating thought and action, team members should come from wide range of backgrounds. First of all, a good team includes representatives of both genders, women and men. I am not in favour of gender quotas, but at least 20 per cent of the work community should be representatives of one gender. Secondly, the age structure of the team should be balanced. I have coached teams with only 20-year-olds or 50-60-year-olds. In these cases, the team works best with customers of the same age, but it is more challenging with target groups of different ages. The competence and educational backgrounds of the team members should be different. Team members should not come from the same place. There should be introverts and extroverts in the team. Extroverted extroverts can dominate the team's dialogue for several hours. When you ask an introvert who has listened to the dialogue what should be done now, they can wisely condense several hours of dialogue into one minute.

The personality of team members can be measured with various tests. The most important thing is not what kind of test is used, but the most important thing is the open sharing of test results with team members. It naturally helps team members get to know each other and themselves. The team acts as a mirror for learning. The tests are often situational, but the individuals will find themselves in them. A good test for introverts and extroverts is by Linus Jonkman (2019) which is noted at the end of this book.

The traditional DiSC test with its various variations helps to categorise oneself as controlling, impressive, conscientious or stable. There is an app for this, where the types of people are divided into as many as 16 different categories. The book entitled Idiots Around Me (Erikson 2017) uses colours, red (a passionate leader), yellow (an inspiring mood lifter), blue (a calm analyst) and green (a natural team member). This book by Erikson is based on the DiSC test, but according to researchers, its scientific basis is somewhat shaky. According to Erikson, each of us can have several colours. I have made the test myself and found my own traits in it. Can more than two million book readers be wrong? One of the best leadership tests I have made with a team I coached was the Unknown Soldier Leadership Test. Above all, it resulted in a forward-looking in-depth dialogue.

Lundberg's (2011) book The Unknown Soldier and the Art of Leadership contains a leadership test that each member took of one of the teams I have coached. Based on the results, they had the best dialogue of my career in leadership. The roles of team members are best measured by Belbin's (www.belbin.com) team role test. The team role is situational and related to the team in question. Action-oriented roles include shaper, implementer and completer finisher. A shaper is an energetic and goal-oriented leader. He or she keeps the team moving. The shaper does not lose a moment and drives the team to work. The shaper is a diligent and responsible implementer. He or she needs a pragmatic strategy. The implementer implements it as efficiently as possible. The completer finisher is precise and meticulous ensuring a polished and scrutinised completion that has been subjected to the highest standards of quality control. He or she is at his best when finishing things. He or she is primarily interested in the end result of the work and not the journey to it.

Human-oriented roles include co-ordinator, team worker and resource investigator. The co-ordinator is a goal-oriented and steady seeker of strengths. He or she focuses on the goals of the team. The co-ordinator highlights team members and delegates the work appropriately. A team-worker is a flexible and supportive mediator. He or she gets the position of the team in order. He or she highlights the essential work to be made and finalises it. A resource investigator is a curious and enthusiastic seeker of opportunities. If your team threatens to become inward thinking, then he or she will bring up the possibilities of the outside world.

Thinking-oriented roles include plant, monitor evaluator and specialist. A plant is a creative and original problem solver. He or she is a creative person whose thoughts can be difficult to follow. Listen to him or her carefully. The plant produces original, valuable solutions. The monitor evaluator is a calm and objective critic. He or she is the logical voice of the team. He or she considers the team's solutions in a reasonable way. A specialist is a determined and self-directed sage. He or she has in-depth knowledge of their area of expertise. Listening to the specialist is of great importance to the success of the team.

In Patrick Lencioni's (2016) book The Best Possible Team Player, there is another interesting style of modelling. According to Patrick, the best possible team player is emotionally intelligent, humble and hungry. The book also includes an interview framework for

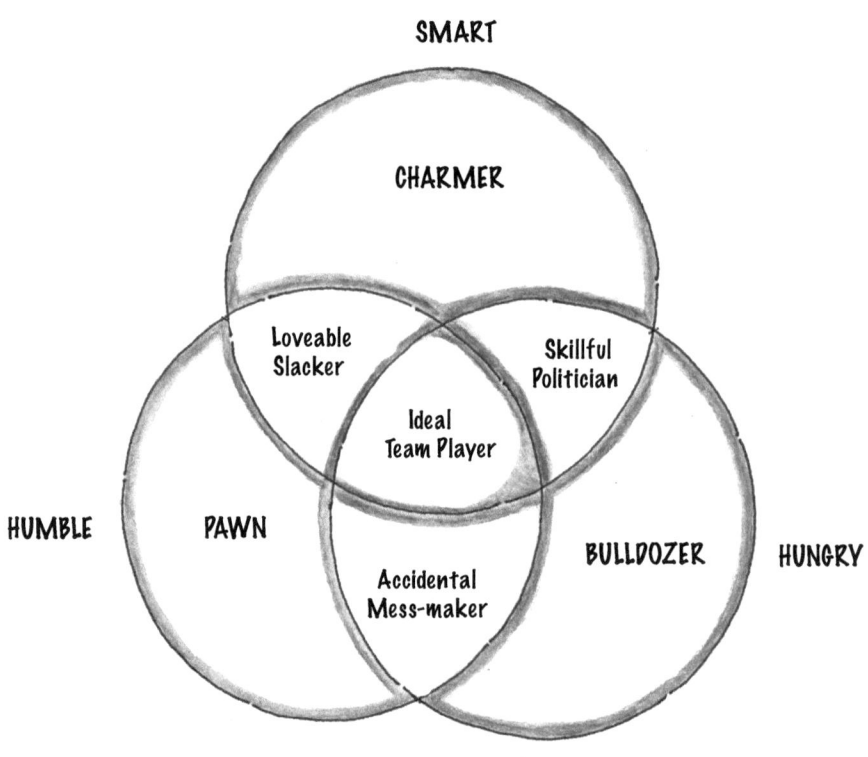

Figure 15. The best possible team player (Lencioni 2016).

investigating the issue. I have used this interview book a few times myself. Once when I interviewed five persons, two of them were the best possible team players, one was an accidental mess-maker, one was a lovable slacker, and one was a skillful politician. There is also another good piece of advice for interviewing a new person: interview new employees at least three times, by three different people and in three different places. I have used this advice and framework in recruiting a new person, because I want the best possible team players on my own team.

In the first stage of teamwork, my tolerance for differences is tested. When a person thinks and acts differently from me, it feels really and truly annoying to begin with. In the second stage, I recognise these differences. Aha, this person is such an extroverted performer, and this is an introverted contemplative. In the third stage, I begin to understand the backgrounds and strengths of the differences between these types. In the fourth stage, I accept the differences as part of my own team. In the fifth stage, we as a team are able to take advantage of our differences and formulate a shared vision.

The first encounter

The kick-off event of a team is unique. When I step in front of the team for the first time, I wonder what I am bringing with me. What is my own character, i.e. my own way of coaching or leading? I cannot start empty-handed, but I think and plan my first steps. My own behaviour and personality must support the team's activities, I am still at the centre of the activities of the team in the beginning and I have to show the direction.

I try to prepare my mind for the start and clear my head of useless thoughts. According to the Japanese Samurai Mushashi, emptiness is the highest level of leadership, and this is where the new begins. I do not know the other people in the team, and they do not know me. I naturally try to find out the backgrounds of the team members in advance. We are always nervous before the start of a new team coaching. There are always two coaches involved, we can support and complement each other, this is why I wonder what my partner is like as we start. We thought about and agreed on the start together. We guide the learners towards the theme of the day with a suitable story or interesting theory and our own personalities. In emptiness, it is essential to find the atmosphere and energy that suits the situation and goals of the team. Team members are in a tense state of mind, so fun and authenticity are important.

Building a team is a long-term endeavour. In the beginning, the key things are a common goal, common time and a fixed rhythm. The common goal of the team must arise from the team. In the name of clarity, it is worth telling the first time why you thought the team existed and why it was founded. Then the team itself formulates its own goal. With time, a very important point is the time we spend together. I minimise formal meetings and maximise informal dialogue. The third very important principle is rhythm –

the team should meet regularly. I would rather have two to three dialogue sessions once or twice a week. Dialogue session begins with check-in, during which we ask how you are doing and how the participants are feeling. Then we will deal with one or two main issues, and then there are the urgent matters. Finally, we end the dialogue session with check-out. We will tell you our own feelings about the meeting and how we feel about moving forward.

Our coaching processes last from six months to a year and a half. We always agree on sessions in advance for the entire time, in particular, in Team Master coaching during two-day encounters at farm tourism sites or remotely are effective. Coaching is based on three things: dialogue, learning by doing, and reading books or listening to audio books.

I plan the start of the team well. I build the learning path for the first weeks first by myself or with my coach colleague. I present my thoughts to the team by putting them at the centre of the dialogue for the first time after check-in and participant introductions. I trust the intelligence of my team and foster its development. My most important task is to build trust within the team. We must be careful in building a culture of trust: the good elements must be strengthened and the bad ones eliminated. Focusing on creating added value leads the team to the right path.

Team trust and communication

I believe in radical openness. As a team coach , I try my best to set an example by telling as much about myself, as well as my faults. Usually, at the stage where there is a dialogue about sexuality or mutually accepted anecdotes relating to it means the trust of the team is in a good phase. If the team is secretive or does not bring up the facts, then trust erodes within the team. As a team coach, I am unable to coach a team effectively if I do not know what is going on behind the scenes. I have to listen carefully to things. Usually, the subordinate clause producing Introvert wisely states the true state of a situation.

Openness creates trust. Another important element of building trust is knowing the others in the team. This is one reason to limit the maximum size of the learning team to about 25 people. When a new learning team starts its activities, we try to work in small project teams as much as possible. A small project team of two to seven people gets to know each other reasonably well even during one Team Leader session. Trust tends to be built through project teams in a large learning team.

Communication within the team creates clarity in the operations of the team. A mutually agreed electronic communication channel used by everyone creates a basis for communication. Such a thing should be agreed upon and arranged. A functional communication culture is created through the example of a team coach. Team communications can be compared to a local newspaper, which is published once a week. The information should be more homemade, aimed specifically at the team and sufficiently regular. The team coach must get rid of the position of the main communicator and transfer the responsibility to the team. At best, a close connection has been established in some team mastery groups, resulting in groups meeting up annually even after the coaching has ended.

Leadership and relevance in the team

The significance of the existence of the team must be brought up in the first encounter. Usually, the team and its learners have a client or clients. The work community that sends the students to the coaching programmes wants results from the learners. The expectations of the learners themselves, others, Team coach es and their own work community clarify the importance of the entire team. This is where the waiting square is formed. A dialogue about expectations gives the first touch of the meaningfulness of the team. The team may also have a clear task defined by the work community, such as "design, build and start a paper machine in China". Even in these cases, getting to know other team members through free dialogue builds team trust.

Building coaching leadership in a team requires patience. The selection of team leaders for the first project teams should be prepared and considered. If I, as a Team coach , have to choose team leaders or junior team coaches I try to suggest good people who know or experience team learning. If the team is formed as a learning team and their leaders change, the first ones set an example for others and lay the foundation for their successors. Team leaders in the work community should also be selected based on factors other than that of subject issues or seniority. I recall how in one team, a dispute arose between the current and former team leaders. The team listened to the dispute in utter confusion. A young team member who had just joined the team then took the lead. He asked the former and current team leaders to settle the dispute in front of others or outside the room. The dispute was settled in front of the team. The team member was then voted as the new team leader when the time came.

A regularly changing team leader builds shared leadership in the team. Moreover, if the project teams have their own team leaders, the learning team can have its own team leader and management team. This is how the Team Academy of JAMK University of Applied Sciences, Proakatemia of Tampere University of Applied Sciences and Mondragon's Team work Academy in the Basque Country proceed. Seamless cooperation between team leaders and team coaches is essential. The transferring of leadership to team leaders is the task of a team coach. The team leader is first and foremost responsible for managing the affairs of the entire team – the team coach is responsible for the learning process of the team. Choosing a team leader too quickly can lead to the wrong choice. An extrovert wants to be the first to be seen, especially in a new team, but is not necessarily the best team leader. Often when an introvert is provided with the opportunity with encouragement, then the team gets a better team leader.

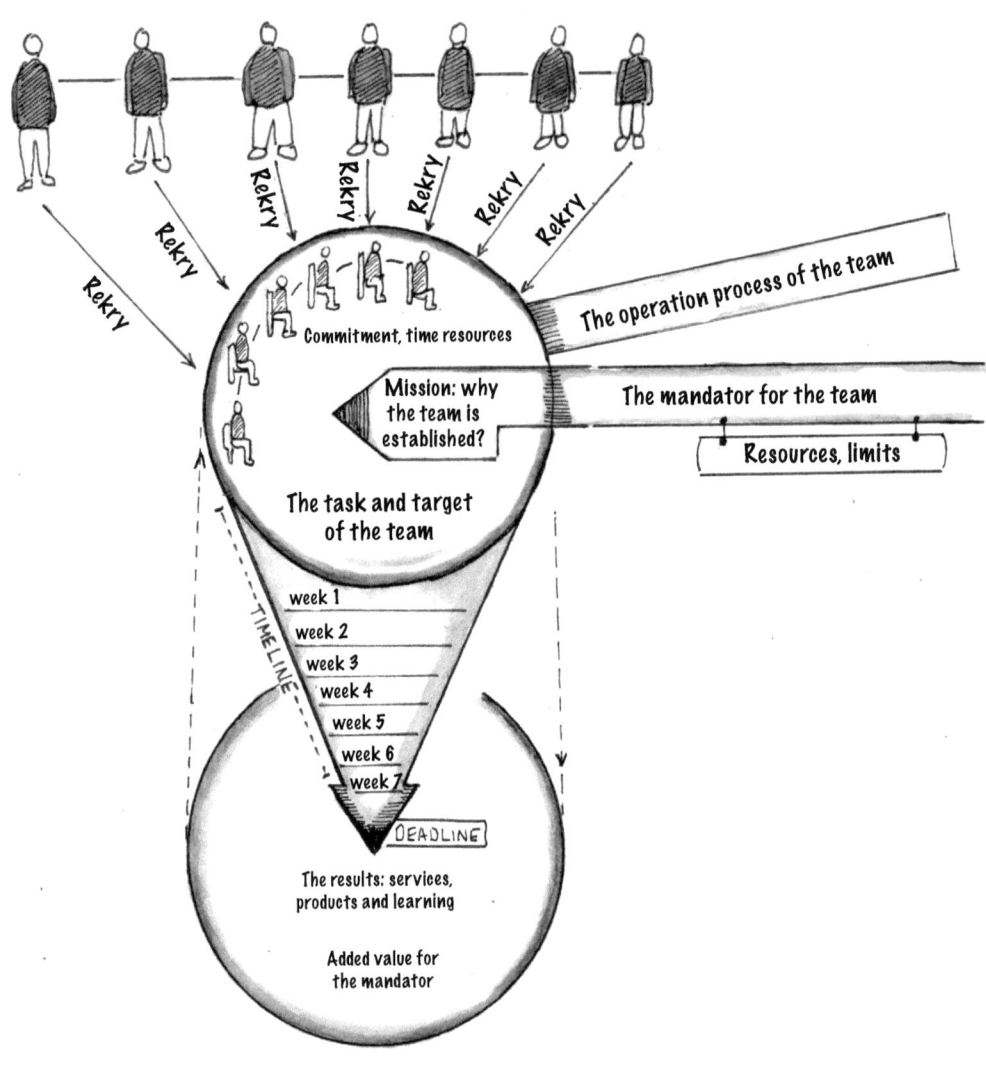

Figure 16. Establishing and launching a team (drawing by Timo Lehtonen).

Effective planning provides a powerful start

My personal experience is from the opening or start weeks at the Team Academy of the Jyväskylä University of Applied Sciences. The concept also works with a new team anywhere and in any environment. During this time, almost sixty new learners started who were divided into three teams during the first week. We had our very own project team just to organise the activities for the first few weeks. The team consisted of new teams, team coaches and the most senior team entrepreneurs (students). My project team created a daily programme for the first two weeks. Along with my working partner, or to put it another way, the rental team leader (experienced team member from previous year team), we planned a ten-week program. This team leader was a Senior Team Entrepreneur who acted as team leader for the first six months.

The following story combines memories and experiences from different years. In actual life, not everything goes according to plan, but some exceptional things can happen, and you can make mistakes yourself.

On the first day, we wanted to organise a personal, mystical and communal reception meeting for all new, freshly selected team entrepreneurs. We invited students to be team entrepreneurs, because each team establishes a co-operative and each new student becomes a shareholder of the cooperative. The new team entrepreneurs first received a glass of sparkling wine and the head coach (principal), team coaches and selected senior team entrepreneurs shake hands with everyone. The welcoming reception area was dimly lit with a dim atmosphere. It was like to arriving at a rock concert at a VIP seat. The new team entrepreneurs were then directed to their places in the front row. The entire JAMK University of Applied Sciences Team Academy was present, about 150 Persons. A band, comprising of all the team coaches, suddenly blast the first song into play, that is to say despite our less than proficient musical skills being somewhat limited and evidently so. Some of team coaches were also dressed as Sheikhs including me and Timo Lehtonen. We had previously bought the sheikh costumes in connection with our Learning Organisation Conference trip to Oman. I could see the excitement on the face of the new team entrepreneurs. The host of the event invited the coaches of the new teams to the stage to introduce themselves. Head coach Johannes Partanen gave a special and in-depth speech about team entrepreneurship. After this, the newcomers had to learn each other's to some acpect according to the Learning Café method, where team learning is introduced. We held the first dialogue training sessions in mixed teams, familiarised ourselves with the customer projects of older team entrepreneurs, and new team entrepreneurs made a presentation on the Team Academy wall about themselves. This event lasted some four hours. Finally, it was then time to give the new team entrepreneurs their two-week program.

We started the second day om a much lower key. We divided the new team entrepreneurs into three groups. One group took the Belbin team role test, another group familiarised themselves the library's services by borrowing their first book, while the third group engaged in a dialogue about the method of team learning at Team Academy. Each team did during the day all three tasks. Based on the results of the Belbin's tests, namely gender, age, professional experience, and local domicile, I divided all sixty new team entrepreneurs into three different teams.

On the third day, the line-ups of the new teams have been published and available to the newcomers. We were now again in the stage area and the event appeared to have a spectacular atmosphere. Each team will work as the same learning team with the same team coach for the next three and a half years. The tension could be felt to our very core. Each team performs with a leader for six months who is their rental team leader. This person receives a turnover based commission fee for their leadership work. Next, the team moved on to its first dialogue session led by their rental team leader and team coach. We started with check-in questions: How are you? Who are you? What have you brought with you today? We listened calmly and carefully through the questions and each individual team member's replies. We have agreed with the rental team leader the script for the dialogue session. This leader then suggests dividing the team into four cells, each with its own function. One takes responsibility for organising the team's home base, another begins to explore the establishment of a co-operative, and the third begins the following week's planned excursion "To the Forest and Back", and the fourth makes a competence map of the skills of each team members based on the first day's presentations. The team has begun to get organised, and the team members get to know each other in more depth. In summary, each cell presents the results of its work. We checked-out of the first day with feelings for the first day.

On the fourth day, the team members started by working in their cells. We agreed the format for the day in that during the morning cell work will be carried out and, in the afternoon, we will have around Jyväskylä Town (the location of the training in Finland) orienteering for all new team entrepreneurs. This included familiarisation with important places for the students such as the Student Health Centre, Main Campus, City Library, Aalto Museum, student organisation and student life possibilities.

On the fifth day, we had a four-hour dialogue session, which had been prepared by the "To The Forest and Back" cell under the guidance of the rental team leader. We needed to prepare for the actual excursion to a local forest for one night that would take place the following week. The second theme of the dialogue session was the introduction of each team entrepreneur and the review of the results of Beldin's team role test. I ensured the creation of a safe atmosphere. In the afternoon, the cells continued their work.

The new week began with the "To the Forest and back" excursion. The idea of this is derived from the book To the Desert and Back (Mirvis, Ayas & Roth, 2003). Our transportation in the form of buses were ready and waiting. New teams with heir overnight wilderness equipment filed onto the buses. We ran a learning adventure, i.e. the beginning of a walk at the beginning of the education year. Each team walked about ten kilometres. Teamwork took place during the walk including tasks that promote information about each other. We arrived at the place where we would spend the night, where we got some dinner and then the three new starting teams organised an evening of fun for each other. We all slept in army tents. The next morning, after breakfast, we collected everyone's phones. The whole group, that is all members of all teams were properly woken with the question: What do you want from your life? The rental team leaders of each team escorted everyone into the forest to sit alone for about half an hour to think about the answer. The rental team leaders brought the group back around the campfire. It was a beautiful autumn day. The sun was shining between the pines. We pondered the meaning of life and each of us have our own answers. We would be going back to Team Academy premises in Jyväskylä after lunch.

On the morning of the next day, the seventh day, each team has a dialogue session. We start as usual with check-in. The "To the Forest and Back" trip is has been evidently effective. The first extrovert, a team entrepreneur who has completed military reserve officer academy training, indirectly expresses interest in the role of new team leader. I pondered in my mind the exemplary performance of this individual during the trip, but I could not envisage this because it is not worth rushing. It is considered best to let the team live normal everyday life before making such a selection. Under the leadership of the rental team leader, the team thought deeply about how the trip went through with the aid of reflection called Motorola questions. Four questions were raised: What went well? What went badly? What was learned? and What should be put into practice? I agreed with the rental team leader to use this after a powerful speech on the launch of team learning: 1) The team needs clients, i.e. learning by doing, 2) Regular dialogue sessions. 3) Reading. The rental team leader presented the program for the remainder of the week: everyone made a preliminary version of their own learning agreement. On Thursday, the first customer visits were to be organised by small cell members. On Friday, there would be a dialogue session where the focus will be on the learning agreements.

When I arrived a little late on Thursday, the cells were already busy arranging client meetings. The rental team leader had asked everyone in their cells to go through their own networks, i.e. acquaintances and relatives. The goal was for each cell to go to visit at last one client in the afternoon. Three cells succeeded in this very well. One cell started to create its own product-based website service and got deeply lost in this activity. On Friday, we delved into learning agreements during a dialogue session, which would reveal everyone's skills, strengths and even dreams. We focused on the following three questions: Where have I been? Where am I now? Where do I want to go? The Rental team leader guided the dialogue session through the cells. In the afternoon we went to the library together and we focused on reading. Everyone had to choose three books that could interest them. Each book is then to be read. We Team coach es were available to the rental team leader if help is needed in choosing books. Books should always be read for one's own needs. If a book does not create enthusiasm, a new one can be chosen and tried out.

The next few weeks went at the same pace. There were dialogue sessions on Mondays and Fridays, and cell meetings on Wednesdays. We prepared the rental team leader with the themes for the following weeks. In the third week, the theme was the establishment of a co-operative, the fourth was friend leadership. In this issue, we divided the cells again. My team itself suggested that we would form the cells according to the themes. The themes agreed were team agreement, customer relationships, well-being and communication. Each cell also chose its own leader. The theme for week five was starting to learn by doing, i.e. customer relationships. Every team member is set a goal to make one customer visit per day.

The theme of week six was a Team Agreement, in which the team agrees on the key rules and goals for the autumn. Everyone was engaged in good workflow. After this, we agreed with the team that it would get to agree on the themes of the weeks themselves as a team.

The theme of week seven was well-being. The team includes a health and well-being team entrepreneur who is enthusiastic about these issues. This enthused team entrepreneur gave the whole team at seven o'clock on Monday morning, a Chinese Tai Chi class. It was outdoors. Following this, we go back indoors for a healthy power breakfast that has been organised by the enthused team entrepreneur, who also talked during breakfast about a healthy diet and exercise.

The communications team members embraced week eight. They were now familiar with the rocket model and created book point goals, monitoring of customer projects and a team strength map on the team wall, according to the model. In addition, the team had created its own website.

The theme of week nine was team leadership. Now the team want to choose a Team Leader and a Management Team. The chosen Team Leader is the well-being enthused team entrepreneur who is a slightly introverted team entrepreneur. The extroverted team entrepreneur who graduated from the reserve officer school became the Key Account Manager, the team agreement cell became the Financial Manager, and the communications cell became the Communications Manager. They together form the Management Team of the team for a year. The theme of week ten was the practices of the team, i.e.

its routines. The new Team Leader had listened to Crear's (2018) book called Atomic Habits and we had a dialogue session related to agreeing on team practices. Dialogue sessions are still on Mondays and Fridays. On Tuesdays, the Key Account Manager gives a customer relationship day program. Wednesdays are cell days and a meeting with the Management Team of the team. On Thursday mornings, there is a reading group, after which the team focuses on their own projects. The rental team leader gradually fades into the background but continues to support the new Team Leader and Management Team until Christmas. We agreed on development discussions with the new Team Leader, which are carried out in pairs. We go through each individual learning agreement

8. Stages of Team Building

Team stages

Katzenbach and Smith (1993) clearly describe the stages of team development first from a group to a pseudo team, then to a potential team, a real team and finally to a High-performing team. In my opinion, this is the best model of team development.

There is clearly a grouping phase involved, and the term pseudo team is especially excellent. The template is simple, clear and in-depth. And the excellent title, especially the English title, Wisdom of Teams, is wise, as is the book itself.

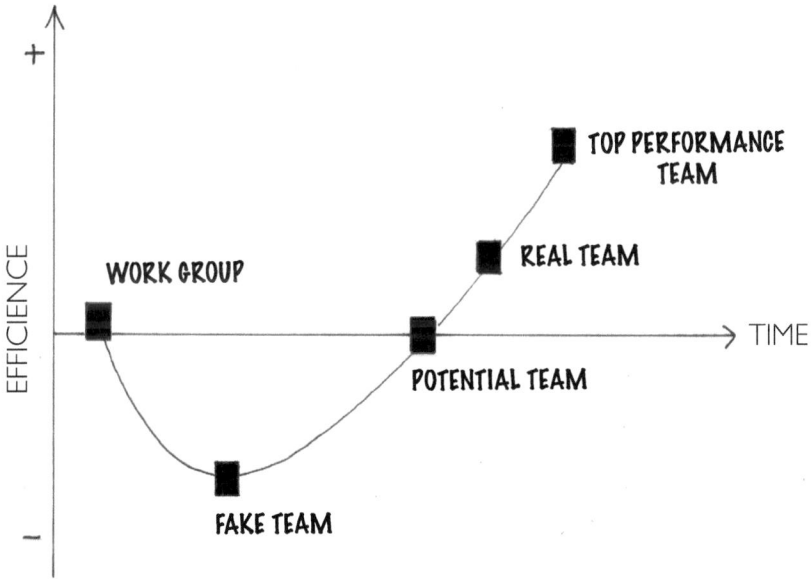

Figure 17. Team Development (Katzenbach & Smith (1993)

When a new group starts, the initial enthusiasm usually engages the team members. New things, new people and a new opportunity are interesting. A group is a group of people who are aware of each other. A team is a group of people who share a strong vision, direction, which the group people strive together. At this point, the task of the team coach is to ask the group: Do you want to start building a team or do you want to stay as a group? In some cases, remaining as a group is a better option if there are no existing conditions for building a common shared vision.

After the initial enthusiasm, the new way of working causes a dip in momentum. We now enter the pseudo team phase. The group does not dare to speak directly to each other yet. Disagreements and failures are not talked about. disagreements and failures No talk. The other team members are still not sufficiently known yet to build trust. The team may seem outwardly functional, but there may be serious contradictions within the team. According to my own empirical observations, management teams, in particular, remain at this point. Leaders compete with each other, sub-optimise their own area of responsibility and do not fully trust each other. If a company has the right management team, as Nokia, the mobile phone maker, had with its Dream-Team, in its golden age at the turn of the 2000s, the entire organisation begins to flourish alongside it. If a company creates a functioning management team, it has a real competitive advantage. At this stage, the task of the team coach is to develop trust, inspire and encourage opportunities. The possibility that the group does not want to form a team should also be highlighted. At this point, a few members of the pseudo team may resign when they comprehend the challenges awaiting the team's journey. This must be accepted.

If the group can agree on a common vision and rules, it has the opportunity to develop into a team. The pseudo team phase is bypassed by building trust. It is built on by talking, i.e. reserving enough time for open dialogue, from two to four hours every week. This is how the pseudo team becomes a potential team. The team members realise the importance of their different roles in achieving the vision and start looking for suitable places to act for themselves and for each other. In the learning team, this happens when the learning agreements have been made. The personal goals of everyone are presented to each other and they form a shared team vision. Personal and team development discussions are good arenas for making learning agreements for individuals and teams. In the learning agreement, the individual commits to the agreed goals, and the work community provides the individual with the resources to achieve these goals. Learning agreement questions also form a good basis for a team agreement.

Effective dialogue is a healthy sign of team development. In particular, the emergence of conflicts is a strong signal of increased trust. Conflicts must be handled and others treated in a spirit of great respect. I remember in particular one Team Master coaching, which involved the management of the work community, middle management and experts. In the civilised and direct dialogue, the pain points of the work community were highlighted, which were talked about in a completely new way. As the dialogue progressed, I kept my composure and did not say anything, but I could not control my expression. One attentive person noticed this even though we were remote, and our cameras were on. The person said: "We need to stop dwelling on this matter and agree on further actions before Heikki's smile is from ear to ear." Even the smile on the team coach can therefore be a crucial method of guidance. The whole work community realised from this comment and my smile that we are now on the threshold of a change. The task of the team coach, at this stage is to help the team form a shared vision and help the team create different scenarios based on it. In general, the team coach should encourage you to think large enough. The team sets its own limits.

From the time I worked as a team coach at the Jyväskylä University of Applied Sciences' Team Academy, many team entrepreneurs (students) have become successful entrepreneurs. For some, it is enough to be able to support themselves, but for others, they are aiming for great growth. The team entrepreneur's own personal enthusiasm and vision are central. I remember well when a Mr. Lasse Jalkanen came to the Team Academy. He had a burning enthusiasm for health foods. He started by importing health crispbread from Germany. Things developed quickly, and in the end, the project's turnover rose to about 500,000 euros during three years of study at Team Academy. Now, the Foodin company, which he founded, has an annual turnover of about 10 million euros. Lasse was an entrepreneur who himself had a clear vision. His own learning team had problems absorbing this, whereas I could not support it enough. The power of vision is enormous.

The team becomes a real team when the team members really perceive the benefits and advantages of the team. The team produces results, and the team members are committed to the team. They notice that the team is a winning group. Results are achieved when the roles of team members are divided according to their strengths and where differences are accepted. In the Team Master group, we normally reach this level at the end of the process. It is actually a bit surprising that twenty learners who are strangers to each other learn to trust each other and encourage each other to achieve results during the process of a year and a half.

Team Master group members fully support any team member if he or she is having a difficult moment in life. In one team, a member developed severe brain cancer. The team member soldiered on and worked remotely several times in a hybrid structure, i.e. sometimes in person and some remotely, according to treatment requirements. Once, when the member was in isolation at the hospital for chemotherapy, the Team Mastery coaching actually inspired the member giving strength to continue battling the cancer leading to surviving the cancer. The feeling when the member had gone into remission and was able to finally be with the team again in person was quite overwhelming. A few times during the learning journey, team master learners have become the award-winning supervisor or expert in their own work community. In the Great Place to Work leadership survey, the leadership results of one supervisor improved over threefold from 16 per cent to as much as 53 per cent in different areas. At this level of team development, team coach themselves notice that their role takes a sideline position: The team coach becomes akin to an observing parent who watches their young ones play. You can ask him or her something, but you do not necessarily ask him or her anything.

Top teams are rarely created. This level is perhaps reached by some five to ten percentof teams. From my point of view, a High-performing team is created when its dialogue flows excellently and the team learns by performing superior actions that can be measured through learning theory (Nonaka & Takeuchi 1995). When the four elements of dialogue, i.e. expectation, respect, direct speech and listening, are met, the prerequisites for forming a High-performing team are in position. However, a team is not a High-performing team until it achieves great things and learns from them. If a High-performing team lacks the humility to learn and openly make mistakes, then it cannot be considered a top team. A High-performing team usually has sufficiently diverse people who know how to use their differences skilfully. The most important task of a team coach is to be consciously present and support the team at the correct moments in the correct way. For a team coach, the law of intervention is central. A High-performing team knows where it is going and how. The team coach's own rants can only interfere with the direction of the team.

Looking back, I recall when a learning team became a top team. Johannes Partanen and I coached the Team Master group. I worked in this as a second assistant coach. The members of the group came from very different backgrounds, including top musicians, teachers, entrepreneurs, leaders, artists, experts and team entrepreneurs (students). By all other indicators, the group was very heterogeneous. We went on a learning journey during the customer relationship period at the gig of one of the participants who is a poet and singer named A.V. Yrjänä: I quickly realised his customer tribe at the gig. The group itself decided to organise the last Team Mastery session in Spain. I can confirm it was a memorable team coaching trip.

It is interesting to examine the model of Katzenbach and Smith (1993) through the model of Patrick Lencioni (2002), in which he has described the development of teams through negation:

- The first level is the lack of trust (= group). Trust and its construction is the basis of everything. It develops through authenticity, actions and good dialogue.

- The second level is the fear of conflict (=Pseudo team). People do not dare to speak directly and raise conflicts.

Figure 18. Five levels of activity in a team.

- The third level is the fear of commitment (Potential team). The group only becomes a team if everyone is fully involved.

- The fourth level is avoiding measurement (= Real team). People do not dare to bring their own contribution to the team.

- The fifth level is ignoring the results (=High-performing team). There are no results or celebrations.

In my opinion, visuality supports all leadership, especially when presenting the process of forming teams. David Sibbet's (2011) book Visual Teams has a seven-step modelling of team development. The strengths of this model are visuality and clear descriptions foreach stage of development. In the image presented on the next page, the main features of the model are highlighted. Building teams in practice is a unique, multi-stage and a multi-generational process, so the modelling only serves as a support for thinking for each team, team leader and team coach. Pat Riley's (1993) Winner Within provides the narrative and modelling of the L.A. Lakers' journey to becoming an MBA champion (four times). This really is a great team book. It highlights the different journey of the team to become a high-performing team. Development does not always go according to the models, though! In their books, Erkka Westerlund, Henrik Dettmann and Petteri Nykky offer a Finnish version of their own team models. The film Apollo 13 (1995) offers an interesting presentation in the form of a film about the team-building process that culminated in three astronauts being saved from certain death in space.

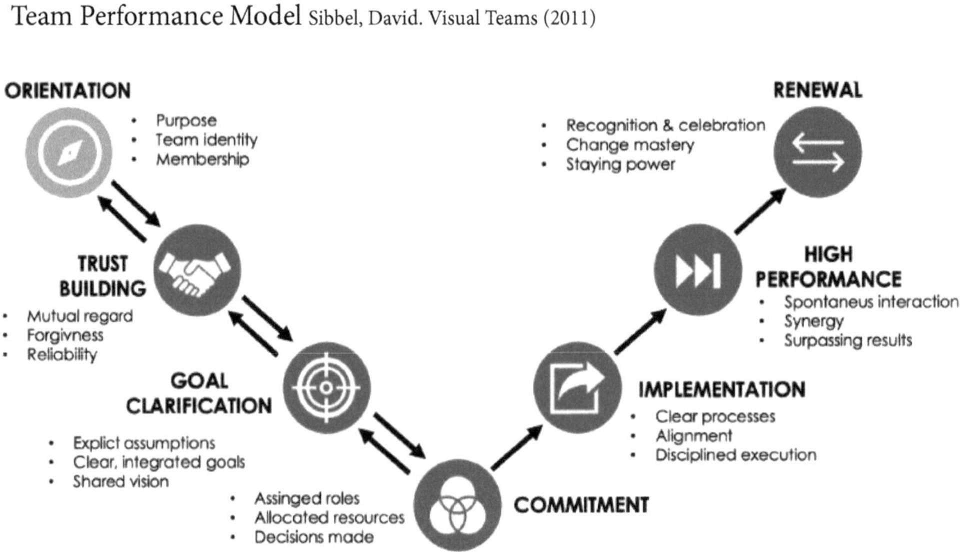

Team Performance Model Sibbel, David. Visual Teams (2011)

ORIENTATION
- Purpose
- Team identity
- Membership

RENEWAL
- Recognition & celebration
- Change mastery
- Staying power

TRUST BUILDING
- Mutual regard
- Forgivness
- Reliability

HIGH PERFORMANCE
- Spontaneus interaction
- Synergy
- Surpassing results

GOAL CLARIFICATION
- Explict assumptions
- Clear, integrated goals
- Shared vision

IMPLEMENTATION
- Clear processes
- Alignment
- Disciplined execution

- Assinged roles
- Allocated resources
- Decisions made

COMMITMENT

Figure 19. Team development.

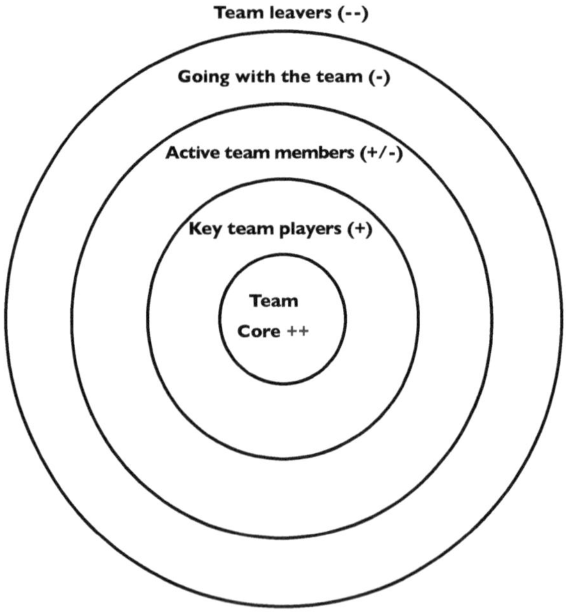

Team leavers (--)

Going with the team (-)

Active team members (+/-)

Key team players (+)

Team
Core ++

Figure 20. Zone theory, or circle theory.

Measuring team performance

An interesting test for measuring team unity is the Rauno Korpi's circle theory (Lehtonen 2012, Korpi 2002). Rauno Korpi is a well-known Finnish hockey coach, who has gained four national gold metals as the head coach in Tappara hockey team. According to the circle theory or zone theory, the team members consist of core team members, key team members, active team members, those going along with the team and those leaving the team. In the first step, I ask the other team members to mark with a dot where they see each team member in their own paper in the team. So, we make a pattern for each of them according to the 20 in the picture. At the same time, each team member thinks of themselves in a certain place in a circle and marks it on their own paper. Every team member will have an own separate. In the second phase, all team members one by one give feedback to each other. At Team Academy, we have combined the test with a one-day coaching session.

I vividly remember one of my team's coaching sessions at a summer cottage. We first performed the test on ourselves. It came as a big surprise to some team entrepreneurs that the team did not perceive them at the core. Someone else was thinking about leaving the whole team, but others thought about him still quite active. The intensive coaching session lasted almost twelve hours. It took less than an hour to take the self-test, but it took from the afternoon to the morning hours of the next day to give feedback to everyone. The impact on personal development and teamwork was hugely significant. The team certainly fused together during this cottage coaching.

Losada (2004) studied top teams through dialogue. Three major axes in the dialogue were found: 1) Positivity and negativity. 2) Open questions and statements (personal opinions). 3) Talking about us and others (customers). Positivity is an essential characteristic of a high-performing team. In a high-performing team, there are six positive comments for one critical comment. Negative comments are important for development, but there should not be too many of them. In a typical Finnish management team, we can talk about a high-performing team when the ratio is three positives to one negative. In a mid-level team, there are two positives and two negative comments. In a low-level team, there are three negatives for one positive.

Another essential aspect of dialogue is open questions and one's own opinions, statements. An open-ended question cannot be answered yes, or no. A good open-ended question wakes up the team, and its effect is long-lasting. The team becomes more aware and to think about the matter from a new and exciting perspective. In a high-performing team, open-ended questions are balanced with one's own opinions. At mid-level and low-level teams, the number of one's own opinions far exceeds the number of open questions.

The third essential characteristic is talk about us and others. A high-performing team talks as much about themselves and others. Their own operations are compared to others and customers are taken into account. In a mid-level team, the conversation turns to oneself with a ratio of 2/3 (others/us). In a low-level team, there are 30 times more talk about yourself than about others. This indicates major internal challenges.

From the dialogue of a team, I am able to tell what kind of level the team is at. I have sometimes followed and observed the dialogue of the team for 30-60 minutes. I have tried to evaluate each sentence or comment through the three dimensions of Losada: whether the sentence or comment was a) my own opinion or statement, b) negative or positive, and c) whether it was about things that concern the team or things that go outside the team. After this, I have presented my evaluation to the team and other interesting observations from the dialogue of the team. From this, we draw conclusions about the situation of the team. The dialogue of the team can be developed by handing twelve cards to all team members: two negative, two positive, two questions, two own

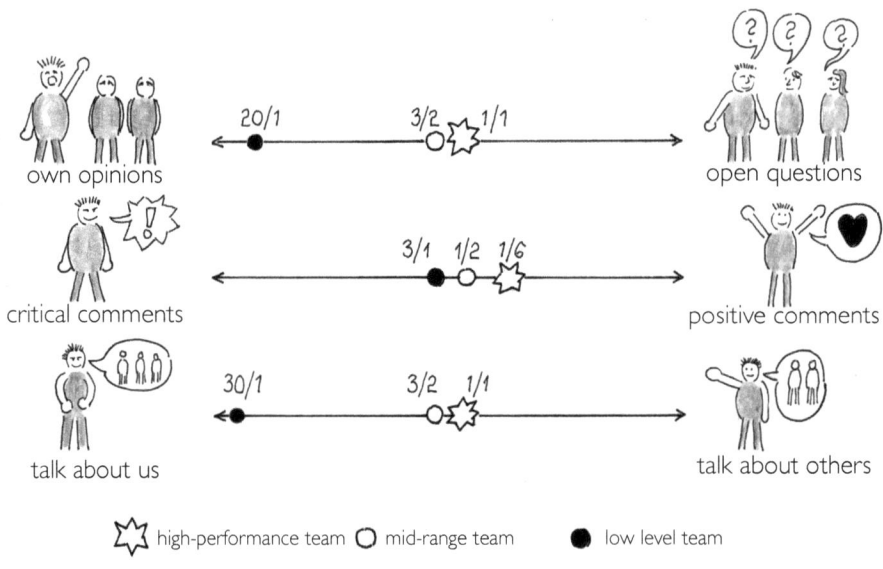

Figure 21. Axes of the Losada test

opinions, two about us and two about the others. When a team member speaks, they put a card on the table. When the first team member runs out of cards, the team can stop and think about the dialogue that took place among the team. Who is talking and what does he have to say? The second version is to make only ten cards for everyone and end the dialogue only when everyone has used up all their cards.

Esa Saarinen, who is a well-known Finnish philosopher, presented J.T. Bergquist's formula at the Finnish Aalto University's Paphos seminar in the summer of 2013. According to Bergquist, teamwork is multiplication. The result of the team is the multiplication of the team members. If even one member joins the team with an 80 percent attitude, the result of the team is 80 percent. A person with a negative attitude can easily influence other members to join in their negativity. If a team has six members and everyone is involved with an 80% attitude, the team's result is 26%. If the team members are able to surpass themselves by 20 percent, i.e. everyone is involved with a 120 percent attitude, the result of the team is 298 percent. The attitude of team members has a huge impact on the team's results.

If someone is not part of the team with a correct attitude, it is the job of the Team coach to raise this issue. I remember one Product Development Team Leader who was involved in training provided by us. The results of the team were measured globally, and the team was the second best in the world. This Team Leader wanted the team to be the best in the world. I presented this formula to the Team Leader. Where upon the Team Leader realised that there were two people on the team who were not fully involved. The Team Leader understood that one of the team members had a negative attitude problem. Being a kind leader, this Team Leader had allowed the situation to simmer for too long. The Team Leader then confronted the person with this issue and found a good solution together with the person. The next time the product development director came to the training with his eyes bright and said: "One more person, and my team will be the best in the world."

9. The challenges and gloom of teamwork

Slow learners

I keep in mind that this is process learning, which means that learning is slow or even slower than you sometimes think. In the early stages of the process, the most important thing is to just listen to the learner who expresses frustration or negative comments. By listening, you can usually find out the root cause of their frustration, after all, everyone is a master of their own learning. A critical or negative comment usually has an important message for the team, team coach or coaching leader. I may be completely incorrect or I have made a mistake while building the learning process. Common reasons for the frustration of learners include a longing for theoretical knowledge, the wrong kind of teammates, and "playfulness and weirdness." The participant may be an uncommitted hangout who feels that the learning process is too slow in terms of usefulness, or they may be forced to participate by their supervisor/work community. I talk to a frustrated learner in private. I usually ask him or her to allow time to themself and the learning process at least during the first Team Mastery period. If the frustration has been caused by other team members, for example, the entrepreneur or manager is in the teachers' group or vice versa, I ask you to give yourself time.

I vividly remember a leader who had been assigned to a teacher-oriented Team Mastery group. The small project team of the leader was joined by one more participant who arrived late. The leader was unable to get a handle on the whole process. The leader was in a fit of rage and very frustrated. I heard afterwards that this leader had called their marital partner in the evening and remarked about going home. Fortunately, the late learner and the leader formed a working pair and supported each other after venting their frustrations. I took them both aside and talked to them and asked them to give them time to learn. Fortunately, both of them did give us time. The leader struggled with the group throughout the learning process. I later heard from the leader's subordinates that significant patience and listening had been learned during this process. With these skills, the leader had made the team flourish.

In some cases, I have been able to switch the learner to another group, in which case he or she has felt that she gets more out of the coaching. I can also change the learner to a different project team. Even in a normal work community, there are always people whose co-operation and friendship are not the most natural. It is good to learn to get along with everyone and to do teamwork. A good team is made up of different people. Differences can be annoying sometimes.

Team learning is based on socio-constructionism, i.e. the learners themselves build the necessary theoretical competence. Unfortunately, our mindsets about learning are often authority centred. We should assume that a more experienced expert can give the information to the learner.

Especially at the beginning of the team coaching process, the learner may feel that the theoretical knowledge is somewhat thin. We have more than 500 different theories related to the coaching process on slides. I do not want to create Team coach -centred learning process. Personally, I am a great non-believer in showing slide after slide. This being said, there are occasionally good slide presentations where the presentation is based on the story and the measurable charisma of the presenter. The best storyteller I have ever heard is Esa Saarinen the Finnish philosopher. The charisma, experience and knowledge of this philosopher create an enthusing link.

The idea behind team coaching is Socraticism. Wisdom is in every person themself. As a feed for learning, I bring out the theoretical knowledge using flip chart sheets that are placed on a wall. I refer to them in my own speeches or sometimes give awareness of a theme that I think the learners need. Every learner should prepare by reading for the periods of team learning. Preparation and literacy bring the flow of learning to team learning. Johannes Partanen has rated the books as one, two or three points according to their difficulty and impact. Everyone should read 40 book points during Team Master coaching. This means 20-30 books, or two books per month. When the learner brings up the lack of theoretical knowledge during the coaching process, I ask where they need theory, how they are prepared and how I could help them. In addition, Team Master participants must collect 40 action points for developing their own activities and 20 community points for participating in various encounters.

Team coaching is based on dialogue that occurs in a large learning team and smaller project teams. According to the theory of knowledge, the project team crystallises its own ideas into an experimental plan through dialogue, i.e. it "creates" thoughts about itself and learns through this. This becomes the term for team learning, birth-giving, which is the modelling of one's own reading theory, new knowledge and a plan for practical experimentation. We want birth-giving to be experiential, i.e. educational, entertaining, aesthetic, escapist and in line with the spirit of team learning. This follows the framework of experience economics in the excellent book by Pine and Gilmore (1999). Team learning also has a profound effect on learners, with them becoming good friends with each other through the process learning. Those who have completed the Team Mastery coaching through the Team Academy and the Proakatemia are considered to have something akin to their own belief system.

I clearly remember a conversation with a manager who said that he was always annoyed with his subordinates on the Monday after the Team Mastery session. They were said to be "overenthusiastic and too full of all kinds of ideas". I admit that the first time I was really confused when I first participated in the Team Mastery program, or when I went to the Team Academy, and especially when I participated in creation. Regrettable, enjoyment and laughter are still not necessarily accepted in every work community. Learners who become frustrated with the "playfulness and weirdness" parts tend to be in leadership positions of companies or organisations, deep knowledgeable experts, or have a different approach to learning. One can only nod at the negative criticism of the learner in this "playfulness and strangeness" category. If I start to defend our actions, the situation will only get worse. The learner either embraces the joy and fun of learning or sticks to their own style. In reality, the myth of experts is being broken. The information is available to everyone, and everyone can become a leading expert in almost any field.

The slowness of human learning is astonishing. Learners frustrated by the "slowness of usefulness" category want quick results.

In connection with this, I am reminded of Alf Rehn's (2018) story about the book Leadership Conflicts. He had been asked to investigate a manager of a large company who was considered good and bad. His observation of a well-regarded, enthusiastic and eager to learn leader was astonishing. This young leader took a short course or lecture and was excited about it for a few months. This, of course, made a great impression on the managers. The leadership trends learned and introduced during the course, with their new leadership styles and tricks, meant that his department was always in disarray and the staff continuously waited with an element of dread for the latest new "trends". A leader considered bad by the management, on the other hand, was, according to his own department, a predictable, slightly moody but fair leader.

Changes in human mindsets in expertise and leadership are very slow. First of all, if I get something new and inspiring in my head, I notice that my immediate environment resists all changes. Secondly, I should alter my own behaviour through experimentation. This tends to be hard. Thirdly, doing everything new carries the risk of error. Unfortunately, many work communities try to avoid mistakes, and an impeccable stay produces more reliable operations. The pain of the learner in the "Slowness of Usefulness" category is helped by a deep discussion and perhaps the question: What do you want from life and what do you really want to learn?

Those in leadership positions have woken up to the fact that team learning and working in teams are the only effective ways to develop the work community. This can come as a shock to the members of the work community, who are made to understand that it would be good for them to learn teamwork and team learning. When such a learner in the forced into category arrives at Team Mastery or other coaching, the skills of the team coach are put to the test. Usually, such a person is prepared with a Teflon attitude, i.e. "nothing extra sticks to me". She or he is surprised that she or he is unable able to work during the coaching as she normally can during the training. Often, they think they are almost completely ready, and this there is no need to change. A project team that inspires this type of person is the solution. Its composition is important in coaching. In a small team, you cannot escape yourself and your own need to develop. Another way to get them involved in the learning process is a deep one-on-one dialogue. The theme of this discussion is how the learner wants to progress in the work community and what their personal learning values are.

A team member in the Independent Hangout category is a big question mark in the team. Usually, he or she does not get frustrated themselves, but the team and the Team coach get frustrated with him or her. This type of person has strayed into a team and team learning by some chance. There is no commitment to the process in any way, and they have their own agenda. Underneath the harmless exterior, there is usually a strong heart that is looking for its own direction. As long as this person finds his or her own direction, nothing can stop them. My teams have included a beauty contest winner, a global citizen, a persistent seller, an enthusiastic artist and an entrepreneur who makes the world a better place. Drawing up the learning agreement properly and discussing it openly in the team helps to find your own direction. If the personal agenda and the agenda of the team, then he or she is a very valuable resource for the team. The team coach must be careful that a person who is used to performing does not monopolise the airspace with their own issues and drama.

The twisted mindset of the whole team or team coach

Sometimes team coaches can find themselves in rather absurd situations. This can happen, in particular, at the very beginning of the team building process or in a team with a strong identity. The team may surprise and come up with a thought or plan that would not have occurred to the team coach or coaching leader at all.

You always have to remember the possibility that the team is completely correct, and I myself have been on the wrong tracks.

If the plan is related to customer acquisition or customer relationships, I think the only way is to encourage the team to try out the idea with the customer. Experiments drive the activities of the team and test the functionality of the idea. Sometimes experimentation can lead a team on the wrong tracks. I recall when I was writing a visual enthusiasm book for friend leadership and one of my own teams got so excited about it that they decided to be without leadership and a leader for some Time. My tasks changed and I had to transfer the team to another team coach. That was the salvation of that team, as the new team coach was able to rebuild the management system for this team.

In the early stages of the process, the entire team can be so confused that they confront the team coach, questioning everything, and I mean everything. The team can have a strong person whose mindset does not fit into team learning, and this person has suf-ficiently influenced the whole team who are with him or her. Or, I have made a serious mistake in the process myself. In this case, it is important to listen exactly what the team has to say and with absolute accuracy. In team learning, overnight coaching is important, because it allows non-formal learning to get going. We deliberately work long hours. I remember one time when a whole team of twenty-five learners suggested in the evening that enough was enough. They asked almost angrily: "What is the purpose of you team coaches when we have to do everything ourselves?" In this, in my opinion, I had succeeded really well when the entire work community started to take responsibility for their own actions. They had to be listened to, allowed concessions and promised more structure and information for the next day. The team coach must create enough structures in which the team feels safe. I had, in this situation, failed at this.

In another training, there was a work community leader, who at the end of the dialogue topic, summarised and presented the next steps themself. My team coach partner pointed this out very elegantly, but with the consequence of the leader of the work community announcing an immediate departure for home.

We succeeded in managing to calm this leader down with the leader promising to stay the night. We then talked the issue over in the sauna in the evening and the leader then promised to stay for the whole coaching. The challenge in this work community was the hierarchical leadership model. Despite the challenges, the leader decided to continue their own development and went to the Team Mastery coaching, challenging themself in real earnest. Since then, the hierarchy has been replaced by dialogue in the leader's work community. This process has taken about five years and now his unit in the whole Company Group receives the best work community and management feedback in the entire Company Group.

An experienced team with a strong identity can have strong personalities who battle with each other. Their personalities simply do not fit together. In this situation, the team coach should get these people to genuinely talk to each other.

One learning team had a member with a strong entrepreneurial personality with a very strong vision of their own development. This person is a typical creative entrepreneur who worked more or less strictly in accordance with the rules. This person's contribution was so strong that as much as half of the team's result was due to the efforts of this person. The team also had one very pedantic and highly principled person with the firm belief that the team was everything. Everything had to be carried out for the good of the team. The chemistry between these two individuals did not match at all and as the team coach I tried with great effort to mediate, but the team made the decision to eject the creative entrepreneur from the team. To this day, I am still very disappointed with this outcome because I genuinely think it was the wrong decision. On an good note, the creative entrepreneur has succeeded very well in their career but failed to complete her degree and graduate.

Special situations within the team

If the dialogue or actions of the team violate the values of the team coach, or if the safety of the team coach is threatened, I will react immediately. Special team personalities can be a large challenge. Once, there was a person in our training who had been found guilty by a court to a serious crime and had actually been in prison for the crime. The background of this person had not been disclosed to other team members and coaches, citing the protection of privacy act. Because in team learning the community is close-knit, someone had found out about the background of the individual and divulged the information the other team members. This immediately created a crisis of trust within the team community. However, the individual worked hard to rebuild the trust to such extent that the crisis of trust was overcome. Personally, I trust the legal system and the judiciary. With people, they have to be given a new chance. In retrospect, the situation might have been different. Data protection clauses, especially the new GPDR system (General Data Protection Regulation, EU 2016/679), protects the data of a private person very strictly. Everyone decides for themselves what information they provide and how their information is used. A team coach must always take data protection into account in their own coaching. As trust grows, learners tell very personal things in the community of trust, so I always mention confidentiality and GPDR at the beginning of the coaching. I have never had any challenges with information matters.

Fraud in teams is extremely rare, but it can happen. I have heard of such a thing a few times in the field of team learning. In one case, a member actually managed to embezzle part of the money of the team. In another case, a summer project was a total financial disaster, and the rest of the team was left in the dark about it and afraid to tell about it. Whenever there are people outside the team involved in a project in significant roles, the alarm bells of the team coach must ring. This is what happened in this case. In the third case, a project just grew too quickly and unprofitably, with the project members outside Team Academy not taking care of their share of the costs. The project actually went bankrupt. The team learners paid off the debts totalling almost 100,000 euros in student loans and continued their studies. At least two of these people are very successful entrepreneurs today. I can only admire that kind of courage and action. Another other reason why I believe in extreme openness. Openness and measurement in financial matters build trust. Another important lesson for a team coach is that the team itself bears financial responsibility for its own actions. The coaching manager, on the other hand, is involved in the business operations and also takes responsibility.

Sometimes direct talk can culminate in a real argument in the team. The team coach has to play the role of a referee. Now it is important to remember the rules of the game, i.e. team agreement and the rules of the team. If they have not been agreed, it is high time to do so.

It would be much easier to make these before the inflamed situation. Lesson: Coach the team to make a team agreement and the rules of the team right at the beginning of the activity. It is very important for the team coach not to choose sides in an argument, because then he or she loses the opportunity to act, and the team can be split in two. Mediating an inflamed situation requires time and patience. It must follow the rules of dialogue: direct speech, respect, listening and waiting. I do not believe in a range of tricks, but one way to start an honest dialogue is to get the parties in the conflict into an aquarium dialogue. There are a few chairs in the middle of the actual dialogue circle, where only sitting in them allows the person or persons to talk. Personally, I have put three chairs in the middle: one for the first opponent, the second for the second, and the third for myself. I open the dialogue between them and follow it for a little while. After this, I move to the outer ring to the dialogue circle and leave my own chair free. Anyone in the team who has something to say can then sit in it, remembering only those in the middle can speak. When the speakers in the aquarium have said what they have to say, a large dialogue circle is formed. Open this with questions such as how to proceed, what is it about or what you think, the team coach can open a dialogue. For him or her, a passive and observing role is probably the correct approach. The team must learn to solve its own problems.

When the team forms a community of trust, it is easy to start sharing very painful personal experiences from the past or present. This is a special situation where the team coach must be careful.

According to the seventh law of the Team coach, the law of intervention, the Team coach must understand, hug and encourage. I myself have been in demanding situations, including: A learner has divorced, a loved one has been dying or died during coaching, a learner has been dismissed, the learner has had a very serious illness, alcoholism, announces that they are having a child (it may be a painful situation for someone else) or that they are getting married. I have acted in such a way that I hug the person and ask: "Do you want to continue in the dialogue?" Usually, the answer is yes. In a moment of pain or joy, a person wants to be with others. The situation must not then be allowed to monopolise the session because team learning is not therapy. Various experts exist for such. This is what I have reminded people when the pondering of painful issues has continued. I remember a case that happened to a team coach colleague where team members started to discuss the painful past issues of the team learners in connection with the termination of a learning agreement. Suddenly, the whole team only had painful things that were being discussed in dialogue. It should be remembered that dialogue is also used as a form of treatment, as in the treatment of alcoholics in the so-called Minnesota method, but in such cases the therapist is a professional in the field of treatment and a team coach of learning.

Combating gloom

Law number five of the team coach is very important. You are more than an acquaintance, but less than a close friend. This enables the team coach to think independently of the team. They must be able to be close to the team, but sometimes they must also be able to look at the team and team members from a distance. In one of his books, Jim Collins describes precisely this. Coaching leaders need to look at the team sometimes closer, sometimes further away and from a different perspective (zoom in, zoom out). Even though J.T. Bergquist's formula says teamwork should be multiplication, in some cases teamwork seems to be the addition of 1 + 1 = 1 or $\frac{1}{2}$, or something to this effect.

Especially in the early stages of the team, the team is so lost that the team coach must also be in the position, if necessary, of the team leader. A team coach creates a learning culture. In terms of team development, it is easier for him or her to be strict at the beginning and loosen the learning discipline later. This is a difficult place for me. Johannes Partanen, the founder of Team Academy, knows this perfectly. I admire how he is able to create a culture of reading in his own team. He really knows how to wake up the team when needed. Settling outside the team, or "zoom out", is an extremely important and useful skill for a team coach. It is good if you can say to the team: "It is okay, this has happened before, you will get out of this." After saying this, the true ability of the team coach is measured. You need to find out why the team is stuck and how can you coach the team forward and take the next step.

You also have to be careful when setting a team goal: "You have to be careful of what you want when you get it," said the rockstar Andy McCoy. There can be different goals: 1) Ones that are necessary for the survival of the team and the work community. 2) Those that are not necessary, but great to achieve. Personally, however, I believe that one clear goal is better than five hazy ones. Goals must arise from the team, and they must be inspiring. The 10 X Rule book (Cardone 2011) reflects on the setting of high enough targets. According to Grant Cardone (2011), with the same effort, you can achieve a goal ten times greater. Healthy self-confidence of the team and its core players is crucial. I have noticed that in capital city regions, such as Helsinki or Tokyo, college students or residents seem to have a slightly higher level of courage than others. There exists the word "world citizen spirit" in these regions. In modern times, spreading one's own activities can be really fast globally, but it requires vision or courage.

Opening the team's eyes to opportunities may not be possible with the team coach alone. A visit to a dream place in the work community or a sturdy expert visitor can get the team quite fired up.

I remember well my study trip to Japan during my studies. Tokyo was so different and it is fascinating that I wanted to work there. Before that, I had to learn how to do things in English and get to know Japan. I finished my master's thesis related to Japan and got my first workplace there. An insightful book can also provide a great source of inspiration.

In my opinion, the number of errors and failures is an important indicator to describe the challenges of the team. If the team proceeds without making make mistakes, then this reveals the goal is too obvious and easy. Conversely, if the team proceeds and continues to make mistakes, then the goal is too challenging. In my opinion, tolerating mistakes at an appropriate level and, above all, dealing with them openly are central to the development of the team. A leader must set an example in this and openly discuss about the mistakes that the team has made. The culture of experimentation is strong when it

Figure 22. Ikigai concept.

is agreed in advance on how mistakes are dealt with and how to learn from them. Jim Collins (2011) wisely advises in his book called Great by Choice that you shoot first with a bullet and then with a cannon.

Keeping the experiment small enough, customer-oriented, measurable, and learning productive forms a circle of experimentation, which Eric Ries described in his book The Lean Startup (2011). His term "validated learning" is ingenious. The work community must establish the places of learning through experiments. A team coach can also assist in helping the team realise where they are. The team should be able to develop its strengths and become the best in its chosen area, and good enough in the areas that just need to be handled. Some of these areas can also be outsourced, such as accounting, programming, marketing, or sales, for example. The hedgehog concept Jim Collins (2001) is a good tool for finding out this core area. The concept works by answering the following questions: 1) What can we be best at? 2) What inspires us? 3) What brings us financial result?

The old Japanese Ikigai concept is slightly more diverse, with the addition of a fourth question namely: What does the world need? This concept is said to guarantee eternal happiness. Ikigai is able to provide one good approach towards the quest for team satisfaction.

Many other aspects of the team agreement and the rules of the operation of the team are related to interaction. Because of this, the team coach or coaching leader's meandering, walking, watching, listening and polling are extremely important. The key coaching method of the legendary English football coach Alex Fergusson (2015) is watching. In work communities, watching and observing the work of team members and learners increases the knowledge of the team coach regarding the team. In small teams and when meeting by chance, meetings are genuine, dialogic and directly serve the needs of team members and learners. The team coach should also be easy to meet, so that the team member gets support exactly when needed.

10. Bring your own character into play

Every team coach and coaching situation is different

We have highlighted the most important trait of a team coach which is the character, i.e. the character traits and the strengths associated with them of the team coach. This can be termed everyone's individual superpower. For this reason, every team coach and coaching leader must know themselves and act through their own strengths. In my opinion, the strength that Timo Lehtonen has developed for himself, i.e. sanding, perfectly brightens his character as a team coach. He says that by laying sand, he wants to ensure that the feet of the team maintain grip in the slippery area of their activities. Timo presents the team with different points of view, tough questions, crystallising visualisations, inspiring goofiness and a caring presence. As a team coach or coaching leader, you get to put your own soul into the game, even if you do not always have time to think about it during the time of coaching. You have to act on instinct. For this reason, the principles of one's own team coaching and coaching leadership should be considered regularly. Making a physical note of them is very important.

The coaching leader and team coach must work with a coaching approach of some 80 percent. It is equally important to work with a 20 per cent guiding approach. The team coach must be especially strict in creating a team structure, which is created from the following building blocks. The structure must have:

1. A shared vision, structure and operating culture of the entire community.
2. Functional learning teams (maximum of about 25 people) and project teams.
3. Communal learning, also known as team learning, i.e. dialogue and learning by doing.

We do not want any team coach to work alone. This is why we work in pairs. We can plan each coaching session in advance together as a pair of coaches.

We will create a script for coaching. We have a mindset of how we think the coaching or dialogue session could go with a few alternative scenarios. When it comes to training that comes from learners, we have to be willing to change the script when necessary. It helps that we can build the coaching together with the coaches of the project team. Casting during coaching is important. While one coach speaks, the other listens, observes, takes notes and ponders the direction of the coaching. In good pair coaching, roles change naturally, and the rhythm of the team coaches is synchronised. I have sometimes had to act on my own due to the illness of my Team coach colleague and at the end of the coaching I was completely drained of energy, because your fellow coach brings space for thinking, confidence in one's own character and guarantees a better result.

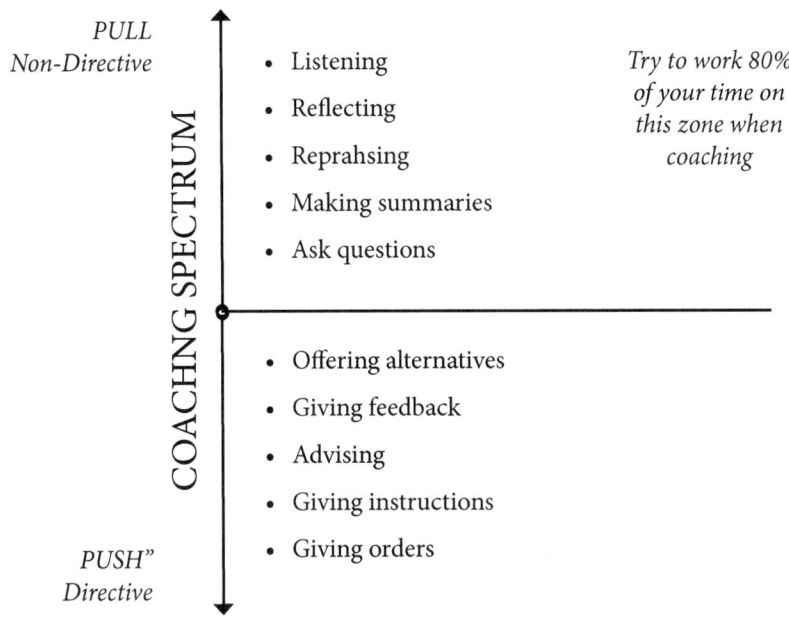

Figure 23. Bringing out one's own character is focused on a coaching approach.

Timing of changing coaches requires continuous learning from the team coach. Finding a synchronous rhythm with a new partner requires an open dialogue about each person's strengths, passions and, above all, character. I remember a few times when preparing for coaching and writing a script required a shockingly long dialogue. I was ready to move forward, but my coach colleague insisted on developing alternatives, ideas and roles. Afterwards, I found out that my colleague was spot on. My own strength and challenge is speed. My preparation could be better for numerous occasions. I can imagine the challenges my own fast, intuitive way of working causes to my coach colleague. Sticking to the script has not been always possible for me because when I get a good idea, I have implemented it right away. I would like to think I have learned to communicate this better these days.

I have been in difficult coaching and leadership positions. In such cases, working alongside an experienced and complementary team coach is heavenly. With some team coaches, the biorhythm coincides well. When a good partner is found, it is worth cherishing the mutual connection and time for dialogue. Therefore, it is worth trying different ways to find good matches. Unfortunately, a coaching leader too often has to work alone. In my opinion, pair leadership is a form of leadership for the future and the present. In a regular company, the CEO and the Chairman of the Board should form a complementary leadership pair with clear roles and complementary qualities. In creative fields, such as theatre, a pair of Theatre Directors is sometimes chosen. The other takes care of day-to-day matters, such as finances, marketing, administration and public relations. The other creates new productions, chooses directors, directs ongoing plays, selects new rising stars for the cast and develops the artistic line. In my opinion, pair leadership is far too little used as a form of leadership. This is one of the insights of the new leadership. Through this approach, leadership can be truly reformed.

The key benefits of pair leadership and coaching are complementary qualities, diversification of leadership and reflection on actions. The team coach and the coaching leader work without delay. When I speak, i.e. I perform team leadership or coaching acts; I cannot possibly observe the reactions of the team or my own actions. When I receive immediate feedback, I can reflect on my actions with the other person and make development measures and corrections without delay. There are many sides to all of us. According to Chinese thinking, we are ruled by two opposing forces, yin & yang, feminine and masculine, passive and active. Complementary pair leaders act according to this ancient Chinese philosophy.

Facilities, home bases and meeting points

The team coach and the coaching leader provide the team with the opportunity to build a space for themselves that meets their goals, a home base and meeting points. Now that remote work is the new normal, meeting points are very important.

I had the perfect remote workstation that was a small room with a window overlooking Lake Pyhäjärvi in Finland, with all the appropriate books nearby and enough wall space for coaching flip chart paper. I very much enjoy working remotely because it allows me autonomy. I can develop personal mastery and get a liberating sense of community remotely without the constant interruption of an open workspace. For us at Team Academy Global, our weekly Monday morning meetings with dialogue are very important creators of a sense of community. This is when we dive into the heart of the dialogue. Everyone is allowed to be themselves. The sense of community is also supported by monthly live encounters. To take care of things, a Zoom meeting remotely is often enough for me. I remember especially well this past winter when we were discussing contracts with an attorney (read lawyer). We went through our business logic and related contracts in depth. The dialogue via Zoom was deep, fast and effective. The rhythm of the meeting points should be regular and weekly.

The home base of the team must be peaceful, homely and safe. A home base is a physical or digital daily meeting place.

Own company has physical home bases in Crazy Towns workspaces in Tampere and Jyväskylä. Presence in the home base of the team must support the sense of community. Typical office cubicles are an extension of traditional, i.e. Taylorism knowledge work. The biggest disadvantage of the cubicles is the constant interruption of one's own work. Spaces for quiet work are critical in offices. I think every knowledge worker can do knowledge work when they want to and where they feel their creativity flourishes. The Team Academy of JAMK University of Applied Sciences is located in a refurbished old factory. Proakatemia at Tampere University of Applied Sciences is by the Tammerkoski rapids in Tampere. It is, of course, my opinion that Tampere is the most beautiful city in Finland, nestled between two large lakes, divided by a large rapid and next to an elevation in the form of a ridge. Proakatemia was located in one of the finest locations in Tampere, and on the top floor of the culturally and historically significant former Finlayson factory, right among various customers. No wonder that Proakatemia achieves excellent learning results. However, I was personally grieved to hear that it had to relocate for financial reasons to the TAMK main campus. To me it is clear that educational institutions are investing in new campuses and their own facilities with little educational results. They have become real estate investors, even though they should be learning communities that empower people. I believe that learning environments should be located in the middle of customers in their sectors: shopping malls, hospitals, industrial plants and farms. The Vocational College Samiedu, in Finland, developed its own new type of forest entrepreneurship degree "So that every forest owner can make conscious choices for the best of their own goals and their forest." The starting point was a hybrid implementation, which includes remote learning in teams and five intensive camps as physical encounters. In this model, there is no need for separate facilities for teachers or students. The size of the learning team is less than 25 people. This is how the team members get to know each other. Samiedu College has become a leading player in Finland in the vocational qualification in forest sector entrepreneurship. Learning is improved and more efficient. The Samiedu College model is shown in Figure 22.

We have ended up holding team coaching at farm tourism locations. They best support our coaching philosophy. Participants can stay in the same place for two days without worry. The learner can focus on themselves and building a team.

This is the best way of achieving the flow of tacit knowledge becoming conscious knowledge. Agritourism locations have many strong benefits for two-day coaching. A good

Our learning model

"If you want to go long – go together"

Thema dialogue sessions and intensive camps.

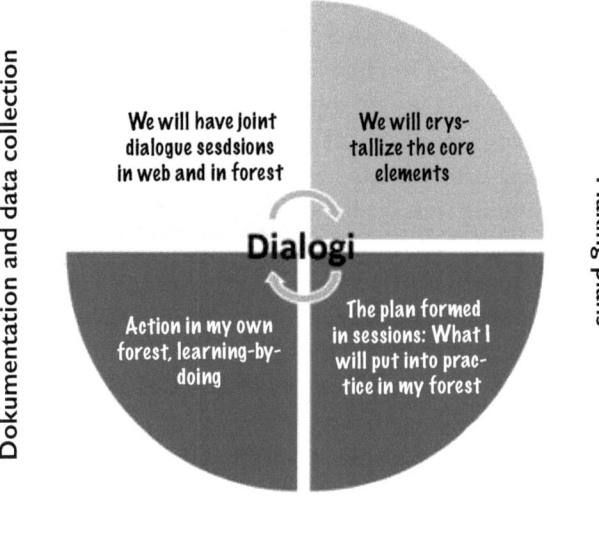

Figure 24. This is how we learn to be a forestry entrepreneur, Samiedu's online implementation.

place has a dialogue space in accordance with feng sui, inspiring small group spaces, excellent local food, an intimate atmosphere, family-like service, diverse outdoor activities and a good sauna world or its equivalent. A good farm tourism place has everything a person needs. The bigger question is how it is possible to build spirit among people inside the working premises of work communities.

Mindfulness – Void

The ability to be in the moment is the most important skill in working life. A person can only be fully consciously present in one place and with one task at a time. In the remote era, this key skill in working life has become even more blurred. Focusing on the moment can be very short, as long as you do it consciously. One CEO of large company has an excellent ability to be consciously present at the time he has promised. He might say, "I have two minutes, what is on your mind?" Then he is really present for the agreed time, really listening. I have read maybe a hundred times in Finnish and English, and listened to Miyamoyo Mushashi's (1654) book "Go rin no sho". There is always something new in the book to find. In it, Mushashi describes the philosophy of the samurai fighter from his own samurai fighter perspective. Miyamoyo Mushashi eventually won all his battles and retreated to the mountains in his last years to write his own fighting philosophy. The concept of void in the philosophy of earth, water, fire, wind and void is very wise to me. Void is the highest level of leadership and a samurai's absolute prerequisite for success in sword fighting. Void means emptying the mind of everything unnecessary at the moment of struggle. The samurai cannot think of anything but a fight, otherwise he will die. In leadership and in life, every moment is important. How could we approach living in the moment in the same way in working life? When we are not present in the moment, can the opportunity of our lives pass us by?

The presence of a coaching leader and team coach also shows that I am committed and care about my own team. If I am away, I have something else more important to do than be with the team. It is a bad signal for the team. Commitment is demonstrated by being present and being well aware of the issues of individuals and the team. Your own attitude and mindset are crystallised in the sentence: "What comes into the room when I come in?" Even though I sometimes have all kinds of things on my mind, focusing on the moment is at the core of team coaching. Buddha is said to have said that we only have this moment and the people who are with us in this moment are the most important.

Sources and book recommendations:

I have marked the title of the book in Finnish, if it is available in Finnish. * marked is Available as audiobooks in Finnish and ** marked in English.

Allen, David. 2001. Getting Things Done. Penguin Putnam Inc. New York, USA. **

Beverley, Grace. 2021. Working hard – hardly working. Hutchinson. London, UK. **

Brown, Brené. 2020/2018. Encouraging Leader/Dare to lead. Wise Life/Random House. Helsinki, Finland/New York, USA. */**

Brinkmann, Svend. 2016. Pysy lujana – elämä ilman self-helppiä. Oak. Helsinki Finland. *

Bungay, Michael. 2016. The Coaching Habit: Say Less, Ask More & Change the Way You Lead Forever. Box of Crayons Press. Toronto, Canada. **

Cardone, Grant. 2011. The 10 X Rule. Joy Wiley & Sons. Hoboken, Ney Jersey, USA.**

Coelho. Paul. Dreams of Santiago (1995) and The Alchemist (2002). WSOY. Helsinki, Finland.

Collins, Jim & Porras, Jerry. 1994. Built to Last. Harper Business. New York, USA. **

Collins, Jim. 2001. Good to Great. Harper Business. New York, USA. **

Collins, Jim & Hansen, Morten T. 2011. Great by Choice. Harper Business. New York, USA. **

Cunningham, Ian. 1999. The Wisdom of Strategic Learning: The Self Managed Learning Solution. Gower Publishing, Ltd. Aldershot, UK.

Clear, James. 2018. Atomic Habits. Peguin Random House. New York, USA.**

Dalio, Roy. 2017. Princeples: work and life. Simon and Schulter. New York, USA. **

Dawney. Effective Coaching.

Dweck, Carol S. 2006. Mindset: The New Psychology of Success (Menestymisen Pyskolog). Penguin Random House, USA. **

Erikson, Thomas. 2017. Idiots around me. Atena Kustannus Oy. */**

Fergusson, Axel with Michel Moritz. Leading. 2015. Hachette Book Group. New York USA.

de Geus, Arie. 2002. The Living Company. Harvard Business School Review. Boston USA.

Hamel, Gary. 2007. The Future of Management. Harvard Business Reniew Press. Boston, USA.**

Hess, Edward D. 2014. Learn or Die: Using Science to Build a Leading-Edge Learning Organization. Columbia University Press. New York, USA. **

Holmes, Chet. 2008. The Ultimate Sales Machine. Penguin Publishing Group. United-Kindom, London.

Howard, Ron. 1995. Apollo 13, movie. Produced by Imagine Entertainment. Distribution Universal Picture. California, USA.

Hämäläinen, Juuso & Sora, Henri. 2020. Strategy for everyday life with the ORK model. Helsinki Region Chamber of Commerce. Helsinki, Finland.

Isaac, William. 1999. (Dialogue: The Art Of Thinking Together skills). Crown Business. New York, USA.

Jonkman, Linus. 2019. Introverts – the silent revolution of the workplace. Athens Kustannus Oy. Jyväskylä, Finland.

Kahneman, Daniel. 2011. Thinking, Fast and Slow. Farrar Straus and Giroux. New York, USA.**

Kangasvuo, Jenny; Pulkkinen, Jonna & Rauanjoki, Katri. 2018. The Revolution of Kotvimisen mous. Karisto Oy. Talliina, Estonia.

Katzenbach, Jon & Smith, Douglas. 1993. Teams and a successful company (Wisdom of Teams). Harvard Business Reviw Press. Boston, USA.

Korpi, Rauno & Tanhua, Pertti. 2002. Yhteispeli työelämä. Thought Books (Gummerus-Ltd). Helsinki, Finland.

Kotter, John. 1996. A Force for Change. Breaks. Helsinki Finland.

Kotter, John. 1997. Matsushita Leadership. The Free Press. New York, USA.

Kotter, John & Rathgeber, Holger. 2009. Our Iceberg is Smelting. Sanoma Pro. Helsinki, Finland. **

Kouzes, James & Posner, Barry K. 1987. The Leadership Challenge. Wiley & Sons. Ney-Jersey.**

Kim, Chan W. & Mauborgne, Renee. 2005. Blue Ocean Strategy (Blue Sea2005). Harvard Business Reniew Press. Boston, USA.

Lehtonen, Timo. 2012. Tiimiyrittäjän arviointipassi. Jyväskylä University of Applied Sciences. Jyväskylä, Finland.

Lehtonen, Timo. 2013. Team Academy – How to Grow Your Team Entrepreneur. Jyväskylä University of Applied Sciences. Jyväskylä, Finland.

Leinonen, Nina, Partanen, Timo (Johannes), Palviainen Petri. 2002. MIA book. PS Publishing. Jyväskylä, Finland.

Lencioni, Patrick. 2002 (2019). The Five Dysfunctional of a Team in the team). Jossey-Bass. Hoboken, New Jersey, USA. **

Lencioni, Patrick. 2016 (2016). (The Ideal Team Player). Jossey-Bass. Hoboken, New Jersey, USA. **

Lombardo, Michael M & Eichinger, Robert W. 1996. The Career Architect Develop-Planner (1st ed.). Lominger. Minneapolis, USA.

Losada, M., & Herphy, E. (2004). The Role of Positivity and Connectivity in the Performance of Business. The American Behavioral Scientist 47(6), 740-765.

Luthans F. & Youssef C. M. 2004. Human, Social, and Now Positive Psychological Capital Management: Investing in People for Competitive Advantage. Organizational Dynamics 33(2), 143-160.

Lundberg, Tom. 2011. The Unknown Soldier and the Skill of Leadership. Positives. Lahti, Finland

Martela, Frank & Jarenko, Karoliina. 2017. Self-management – How to organise a future in the future. Alma Talent. Helsinki, Finland.

Maurer, Bob & Hirschman, Leigh Ann. 2012. The Spirit of Kaizen. McGraw Hill. New York, USA.**

McChrystal, Stanley. 2015. Teams of Teams - New Rules of Engagement for a Complex World. Penguin Random House. New York, USA.

De Mello, Anthony. 1994. Can you hear the bird's song and Wisdom glimpses. Book Workshop. Helsinki, Finland.

Mintzberg, Henry. 1994. The Rise and Fall of Strategic Planning. Prentice Hall. New York, USA.

Mirvis, Philip; Ayas, Karen & Roth, George. 2003. To Desert and Back. Jossey-Bass. San Francisco, USA.

Mushashi, Miyamoyo. 1654. Go rin no sho (A Book of Five Rings , Victor Harris 1974, Earth, Water, Fire, Wind and Emptiness), Samppa Lahdenperä 1983. Big Dipper. Keuruu, Finland. **

Nair, Summer Saw. 1995. A Higher Standard of Leadership: Lessons from the Life of Gandhi). Information message. Helsinki, Finland.

Nissinen, Vesa. 2004. Deep Leadership. Talentum. Helsinki, Finland.

Nonaka, Ikujiro & Takeuchi, Hirotaka. 1995. The Knowledge-Creating Company. Oxford University Press. Oxford, UK.

Partanen, Johannes. 2019. What does a team coach need to know about innovation? Team Academy Global Oy, Jyväskylä, Finland.

Partanen, Johannes. 2022. Focus on the customer. Team Academy Global Oy, Jyväskylä, Finland.

Partanen, Johannes. 2022. Sales and marketing. Team Academy Global Oy, Jyväskylä, Finland.

Partanen, Johannes. 2023. Book of books 2022-23. Team Academy Global Oy, Jyväskylä, Finland.

Partanen, Johannes. 2012. Team coach's Best Tools. Partus Oy. Jyväskylä, Finland.

Partanen, Johannes. 2014. Glimpses of individual learning. Partus Oy. Jyväskylä, Finland.

Partanen, Johannes. 2020. Book of books. Partus Oy. Jyväskylä, Finland.

Peters, Tom. 1982. In Search of Excellence. Harper & Row. San Francisco, USA.

Peters, Tom & Austin, Nancy. 1989 (1985). A Passion for Success Excellence). WSOY. Helsinki, Finland.

Peters, Tom. 1989. Driving on Chaos (1989). Breaks. Helsinki, Finland.

Pine II, Joseph B. & Gilmore, James H. 1999. The Experience Economy. Harvard Business School Publising. Boston, USA. **

Prashnig, Barbada (1997). Long live diversity. A revolution in learning. Atena. Jyväskylä, Finland.

Pirsig Robert M.1974. Zen and motorcycle maintenance. WSOY. Helsinki, Finland.

Quinn, Feargall. 1990. Crowing the Customer. Kauppiaiden Kustannus. Helsinki, Finland.

Rehn, Alf. 2018. Leadership Conflicts. Associate professor. Jyväskylä, Finland. *

Ries, Eric. 2011. The Lean Startup - How Today's Entrepreneurs Use Continuous

Innovation to Create Radically Successful Businesses (Lean Startup) handbook). Random House. New York, USA. */**

Riley, Riley. (1993). The Winner Within. Berkley Books. New York, USA.

Ristikangas, Marjo-Riitta & Ristikangas, Vesa. 2010. Coaching leadership. WSOYpro. Helsinki, Finland.

Robbins, Mel. 2017. The Second Rule. Savio REPVBLIC. USA.

Roddick, Anita. 1991. Body & Soul. Thorsons Publishers. London, UK.

Roddick, Anita. 2000. Business as Unusual. Thorsons Publishers. London, UK.

Saari, Oskari. 2016. Aki Hintsa – The Anatomy of Winning. WSOY. Helsinki, Finland. *

Saari, Oskari. 2020. Petteri Nykky – The Road to Success. WSOY. Helsinki, Finland. *

Saarikoski, Saska. 2017. Henrik Dettman and the Skill of Leadership. WSOY. Helsinki, Finland.

Sahlberg, Pasi. 2015. The success story of a Finnish school. Intokustannus Oy. Helsinki-Finland.

Salminen, Jari. 2013. Skilled team coach. J-Impact. Helsinki, Finland.

Senge, Peter. 1990. The Fifth Discipline: The Art and Practice of the Learning Organization. Doubleday/Currency. New York, USA.**

Senge, Peter. 1999. The Dance of Change. Doubleday/Currency. New York, USA

Sewell, Carl.1990. Customers for Life. Peguin Hause. New York, USA.

Soback, Dan. 2021. Coaching Leadership. Basam Books Oy. Helsinki, Finland.

Stanier, Michael Bungay. 2016. The Coaching habit: Say less, ask more and change the way you lead forever. Box of Crayon Press. **

Sutinen, Mika & Kuitunen, Mikko. 2018. Awesome mistake. Alma Talent. Helsinki Finland.

Toivanen, Heikki. 2013. Visual Inspiration Book for Friend Leadership. Pellervo. Helsinki, Finland.

Tracy, Brian. 2002 (2017, 3rd edited version). Eat that frog. Berrett-Koehler Publications. Oakland, California, USA. **

Tuominen, Saku. 2014. Creative Rationality – Everyday Creativity Crossing. Big Dipper. Helsinki Finland. *

Turtola, Martti. 2016. Mannerheim. Tammi Publishing Company. Helsinki, Finland.

Tzu, Sun. 500 BC. The Art of War. In English in 1963

Samuel B. Griffith, in Finnish Heikki Karkkonen 1998. WSOY. Helsinki, Finland.

Urzelai, Berrbizne & Vettraino, Elinor (edited by). 2021-2022. Routledge Focus is Team Academy: 1. Team Academy and Entrepreneurship Education; 2. Team Academy: Leadership and Teams; 3. Team Academy in Diverse Settings; 4. Team Academy in Practice. Routledge. Milton Park, Abingdon, Oxfordshire, UK.

Westerlund, Erkka. 2019. The Game of Life. Fitra. Helsinki, Finland.

Wickman, Gino & Winters, Mark C. 2015. Rocket Fuel. BenBella Books Inc. Dallas, USA.

Wilenius, Markku. 2015. The Book of the Future. Big Dipper. Helsinki, Finland.

von Wright , Henrik. 2002. My life as I remember it. Big Dipper. Helsinki, Finland. Appendix 1.

The background theories of the Team Academy include at least the following books:

Peter Senge highlighted learning organizations with his book 5th Displine (1990). Dance of Change, Peter Senge (1999) highlights the importance of teams in building learning.

Ian Cunningham (1999) highlighted the learner's own responsibility for their own learning and presented The Wisdom of Strategic Learning.

Dryden & Voss (1997), in The Revolution of Learning, pointed out the importance of lifelong learning principles.

Barbada Prashnig (1997) emphasises the importance of diverse learners in her book Long Live Diversity – a revolution in learning in practice.

The title of the book, Dialogue and the Art of Thinking Together (Willam Isaacs, 1999), is one of the best I have encountered – and the content is ironclad.

Katzenbach & Smith (1993), in their book Teams and a Successful Company, describe the theory.

Pat Riley (1994) tells The Winner Within in practice how to build a top team in the world of basketball.

Kouzes & Posner's (1987) book The Leadership Challenge lays the foundation for peer leadership development at Team Academy.

John Kotter's (1996) book Change Requires Leadership and Nair's (1996) book Leadership The great challenge lays the foundation for the development of leadership at Team Academy.

Finding entrepreneurship and values at Team Academy was influenced by the books by Jim Collins & Jerry Porras (1994) Built to Last; Arie deGeus (2002) The Living Company; John Kotter (1997) Matsushita Leadership and Anita Roddick (2000): Business as Unusual.

The customer has always been at the heart of everything we do at Team Academy. It has been influenced by Quinn (1990) who published the classic book Customer is First – the same book that is the Finnis K-Retail Group's development of its service approach. The classic of the experience economy, Pine & Gilmore (1999): The Experience Economy laid the foundation for the generation of knowledge and customer encounters. Tom Peters & Nancy Austin's (1989) book Passion Anita Roddick's (1994) book Body & Soul and Carl Sewell's (1990) Customers for Life influenced the development of customer thinking.

Nonaka and Takeuchi's (1995) book The Knowledge-Creating Company built a model-for learning by doing and dialogue, which is very central to the Team Academy.

Tom Peters' (1989) book Creative Chaos 1 & 2 encourages the use of chaos in the in the future.

Spiritual growth at Team Academy has been supported by Coelho's books Santiago's Dreams (1995) and the Alchemist (2002); De Mello: Can You Hear the Bird's Song and the Wisdom and Pirsig's (1974) Zen and motorcycle maintenance.

The theoretical framework is constantly being updated as new books are published. The team Johannes Partanen, the founder of the Finnish Book, publishes the Book of Books guide every year, comprising of almost 1000 Best Books that Support Team Learning.

The method of team learning has been defined by Johannes Partanen (2012) in his book The best tools for a coach and Glimpses of individual learning. Team Academy is described by Timo Lehtonen (2013) in his book Team Academy – how to grow your team entrepreneur. My book Buddy Leadership Visual Enthusiasm Book (2013) tells about the leadership model of Team Academy.

About the author of this book

The author of the book, Mr. Heikki Toivanen, Dr. Sc. (Tech.), has a very diverse work experience. He began his long career at Savcor Oy/Ltd, by creating a new business in Japan. His boss who is a relative of a Samurai taught Heikki how to be a businessman and how to good habits. Returning to Finland, Heikki became acquainted with sales work in the same company as a Business Manager.

After joining the global Paper Machinery Technology company called Valmet, Heikki started a new doctor blade business, with a turnover going from zero to more than EUR 10 million. During this period, Heikki succeeded in achieving 20 patents. Heikki worked in global spare parts business management teams in the 2000s. Early on in 2005, Heikki successfully defended his doctoral dissertation on the theme "Strategic logic and gamemanship in the paper and pulp machine industry from the 1970s to the 2000s".

In 2008, Heikki moved to the Jyväskylä University of Applied Sciences' Team Academy as a Team Leader. and Principal Lecturer. During this time, the Friend Leadership - A Visual Inspiration Book was written. In 2014, Team Academy Global Oy then invited him to become the CEO of Team Academy Global Oy and become a shareholder. Team Academy Global Oy has successfully coached thousands of teachers, principals, experts and managers.

FSC

www.fsc.org

MIX

Paperi vastuul -
lisista lähteistä
Paper from
responsible sources

FSC® C105338